The Businessman's Complete Checklist

W. C. Shaw & G. J. Day

Hutchinson Business

London Melbourne Auckland Johannesburg

Hutchinson Business
An imprint of Century Hutchinson Ltd
62–65 Chandos Place, London WC2N 4NW

Century Hutchinson Australia PTY Ltd
16–22 Church Street, Hawthorn, Melbourne,
Victoria 3122

Century Hutchinson New Zealand Ltd
32–34 View Road, PO Box 40–086, Glenfield,
Auckland 10

Century Hutchinson Group South Africa (Pty) Ltd
PO Box 337, Bergvlei 2012, South Africa

First published 1978
Reprinted 1980, 1981, 1982, 1985

Second edition 1987

© Hutchinson Business 1987

Printed and bound in Great Britain by Butler and
Tanner

British Library Cataloguing in Publication Data

Shaw, W. C.
  The businessman's complete checklist.
  1. Management 2. Organization charts
  I. Title II. Day, Graham
  658   HD38

ISBN 0–09–172627–1
     0–09–162671–4 (pbk)

Contents

List of Diagrams

Foreword

SIR PETER PARKER, M.V.O.

There is no doubt in my mind that this book is necessary: it simplifies, it summarises, it insists on the obvious so often dangerously taken for granted, it hunts hard the blessed details. That is the point of the Checklist approach.

Any manager today needs to call on an armoury of skills. First, inevitably, technical competence. There must be a basis of knowledge, by training and experience, which produces the professional skill to combine through administration resources with markets to some profitable end — this is the essential and professional dimension and it is measurable.

Secondly, there is the dimension of entrepreneurial judgement; this is less measurable but crucial too. Here is the capacity for risk taking and risk making which makes all the difference between administration and business. Having looked hard at the selection of options, there must be a capacity still to leap, to land on the preferred option.

Thirdly, and increasingly important in our modern industrial society, is the call for social skills. The social realities are that a manager can only implement the preferred option if he can convince his social partners, i.e. his fellow managers and staff, that his sense of priorities makes common sense. And so it is that business management is nowadays in a context, almost a continuum, of consultation and negotiation.

The value of any Checklist is not that it aims to teach necessarily, but aims to remind and to provide a controlled process for decision making. Furthermore it deploys information in such a way as to establish a logical approach to problem solving. This book seems to me to effectively link the essential skills of management. It must improve the entrepreneurial skill by more clearly evaluating the alternatives offered, and thus more clearly defining the risks. And this lays the foundation for more effective communication in the achievement of consent to action.

For my part this is the particular value of this Checklist; this book forces a full view of the responsibilities of the decision maker in their daunting variety. I suppose there are some people who can dismiss Checklists; all these things they do as a matter of course and logically. Others, more fallible, will draw some reassurance and indeed guidance and, more, a widening of vision. Far too often in our functional and departmental concentration, we lose sight of the size and shape of the wood as we study our own separate organisation trees. *The Businessman's Complete Checklist* reflects the range that is now necessary in the manager's armoury to deal with enterprise 'in the round'. Businessman? Superman?

Peter Parker
April 1978

1 Corporate Planning

1.1 BASIC PRINCIPLES OF COMPANY PLANNING

The purpose of company planning is to create the conditions today for the company to become aware of future market opportunities and to avoid dangers.

It is concerned with four questions:
Where does the company stand now?
What are its goals for the future?
How are its objectives to be reached?
What decisions must be taken now?

Effective planning stems from

Creative thinking
Use of a planning system
Sound knowledge of the company and its market
The choice of different options
Co-ordination

What do you need to know to plan ahead for the company?

Two main parts:
Production of a plan:
What is necessary
What is possible
How it can be achieved
Results of plan

Application of plan:
Management requirement
Controls
Systems
Organization
Monitoring

1.2 PLANNING CONCEPT

Planning can be:
forward
future
strategic
corporate
long term

the motivation:

an increase on the return from effort
the more effective utilisation of resources

Planning of growth needs answers to:

What is the corporate aim?
Why is it necessary to aim or set targets?
Where will the company be if the targets are not achieved?
Who will be assigned the task of defining the aims or objectives, then implementing them?
When should the anticipated plans materialise?
How will the plans be fulfilled and measured?
How much additional resources will be required?

A planning system which has no built-in mechanism to ensure the conversion of both short term and long-term plans to a course of action is unlikely to achieve its purpose.

PLANNING — two main areas

the internal environment
the external environment

Internal environment
materials
production facilities and efficiency
management
labour relations
costs
cash flow
financial resources

External environment
market penetration
market growth
competition
government legislation
consumer change
environment

1.3 PLANNING — THE CORPORATE ENTITY

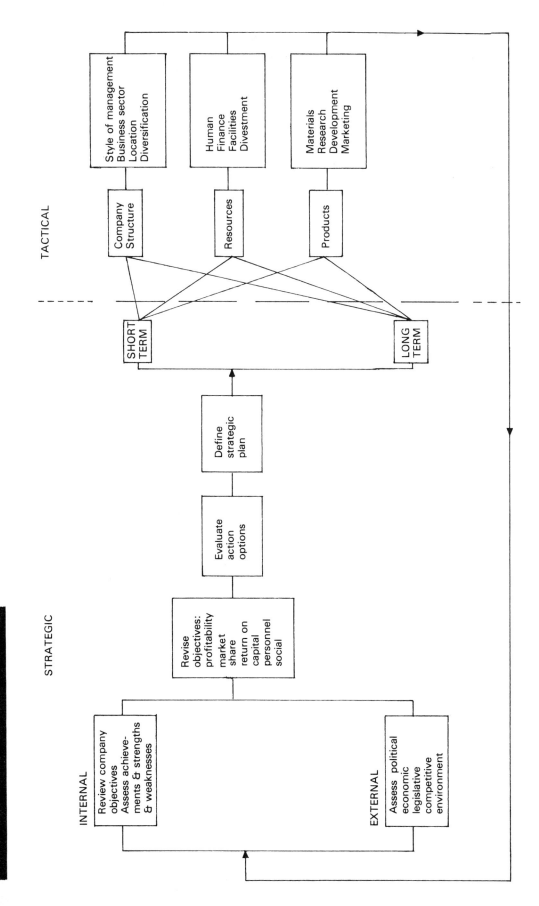

STRATEGIC

INTERNAL

Review company
objectives
Assess achieve-
ments & strengths
& weaknesses

EXTERNAL

Assess political
economic
legislative
competitive
environment

Revise
objectives:
profitability
market
share
return on
capital
personnel
social

Evaluate
action
options

Define
strategic
plan

TACTICAL

SHORT
TERM

LONG
TERM

Company
Structure

Resources

Products

Style of management
Business sector
Location
Diversification

Human
Finance
Facilities
Divestment

Materials
Research
Development
Marketing

Percentage market share — by product and/or territory

Cost of sales force as percentage of turnover

Ratios e.g. return on sales, cost to sales on capital, on pre-tax profits

An absolute level of sales

Minimum acceptable figure for customer complaints

Number of customer enquiries

Maximum figure for productive hours lost

Lead time productivity increases

Reduction in late deliveries

Maximum number of employees

Acceptable level for employee "wastage" rate

Maximum permitted variance from budget

Cost reduction target

Timetable major events

Increase in contribution to overheads

Reduction in debtors as percentage of turnover

Reduction in credit given

Reduction in finished stock levels

More economical work in progress

A *goal* is a corporate, divisional or departmental target, a *standard of performance* is something which is individually assigned to a named person.

The importance of personal standards is that they provide a tool for ensuring that plans are converted into tasks people can do — and are expected to do.

A *corporate plan* involves the setting of *corporate objectives.*

Ground rules affect the attainment of these objectives through

attitude to employers and customers

nature of the organisation's business

attitude to risk taking

attitude towards changing the capital structure

willingness to acquire other companies

willingness to recruit new management generally

Plans

development	*operational*
divestment	manufacturing
diversification	production
new business	capacity
expansion	requirements
research and	marketing
development	sales
	administration
	finance
	manpower
	managerial
	non managerial
	capital expenditure

Monitoring and control

performance summary

analysis of variances

action

revised plan

1.6 THE CORPORATE PLAN IN DETAIL

Introduction
> Aim and strategic path
> Scope of plan and subsidiary plans

Assumptions
> Economic: price levels, inflation etc
> Social: industrial relations, pollution etc
> Governmental: legislation etc

Primary objectives
> Increase return on capital and earnings per share

Secondary objectives
> Area of business or trading
> Market penetration
> Customer loyalty
> Labour relations

Strength and weaknesses
> Raw material dependence
> Product reputation
> Delivery schedule reputation
> Service availability
> New product innovations
> Management structure
> Worker participation and labour relations
> Plan capacity

Statement of expected results
> Quantification of strategies and aims to coincide with primary and secondary objectives

Risk and sensitivity
> Special hazards interacting on probable achievement of strategy

Strategies
> Revision of present strategies e.g. new licencing agreements required to enable sales targets to be met

Operational improvements
> Expansion or rationalisation — creating facilities both permanent assets and human resources

Organisation and Management
> Revision of area of management and administration
> Recruitment policies

Diversification
> Change in procedure of product manufacture and/or sales distribution network

Finance
> Ascertainment of capital to enable plans to be fulfilled

Contingency plan

Criteria for effective planning
> The plan should be concise yet long enough to give a clear understanding of what is intended
>
> All well prepared plans have a purpose
>
> There is always more than one course of action
>
> The course of action chosen must be properly defined, and the reason for the choice understood
>
> A plan must show that the purpose can be attained
>
> Results expected from the course of action chosen must be specified
>
> If the plan is to result in individual tasks it must allocate responsibilities

Timescale
> Complete long range plans in first 6 months of each accounting year to cover either 3 or 5 years from start of next accounting year
>
> The master plan should be rolled forward annually so that a 3 or 5 year plan is available
>
> Complete budgets (or operating plans) for first year of plan during last quarter of preceding year
>
> Every plan should have a timetable attached.

1.7 PLANNING REQUIREMENTS

Planning requirement most needed when:

Capital intensive

Vulnerable to changes in:
Competition
Technologies
New product development

Low liquid resources
Long lead time for change to be implemented
Mature products mainly completing their profit
life
Only moderately competent management
at all levels
Low all round competence
Manufacturing industry
Slow response to competitors' activities
Few products, one or two predominating
Product model changes
Diversification never attempted or attemp-
ted unsuccessfully
Highly administrative to production staff
ratio
Difficult company environment
Future of the company uncertain
Production orientated
Low synergy
Flexible posture necessary for the
company's long term survival

Risk reduction
Choose strategies with lower adverse
effects if assumptions wrong
Devise contingency plans
List hedging actions

1.8 THREE KEY AREAS OF PLANNING

Strategic Planning

Choosing company objectives
Planning the organisation
Setting personnel policies
Setting financial policies
Setting research policies
Choosing new product lines
Acquiring a new trade
Deciding on non-routine capital expendi-
tures

Management Planning

Formulating budgets
Planning staff levels
Formulating personnel practices
Working capital planning
Formulating advertising programmes
Deciding on research projects
Choosing product improvements
Deciding on plan rearrangement
Deciding on routine capital expenditures
Formulating decision rules for operational
control
Measuring, appraising, and improving
management efficiency

Operational Planning

Controlling recruitment
Implementing personnel policies
Controlling credit extension
Controlling placement of advertisements
Scheduling production
Controlling inventory
Measuring, appraising, and improving
workers' efficiency

1.9 DECISION MAKING PROCESS

Define the problem; locate the critical factor

Determine the conditions for its solution, the need to meet objectives and the balance between present and future.

Analyse the problem, find the facts necessary to a solution and capable of being obtained. Know where facts stop and assumptions begin

Develop option solutions, including 'do nothing'

Choose between solutions using as criteria for choice: risk, economy of effort, timing, limitation of resources

Make the solution effective

1.10 SYSTEMATIC APPROACH TO PLANNING

Initial stimulus
    Are you aware of the problem?

Identification of the problems
    Time spent in identifying and interpreting the problems saves money and effort

Quantify the problem and set
    the dimensions
    the priorities
    the resources
    the time levels

Review the available resources
    Have you knowledge, manpower, finance?

Establish numerous solutions
    Consider advantages and disadvantages

Select appropriate solution
    Apart from facts, hunch plays its part through human qualities and experience

Residual problems
    Consider the problems which arise from implementing original solutions

Implement the solutions
    Establish guidelines and monitor progress

Review actions
    Revise procedures

Re-enter planning cycle

1.11 INTEGRATED COMPANY PLANNING

Analysing and appraising the situation

↓

Setting objectives

↓

Assembling possible market strategies

↓

Choosing the most favourable strategy
in the traditional markets or
by diversification

↓

Developing individual plans for sales,
product development, production, manpower,
acquisitions, organisation, finance

↓

Checking the individual plans against the
financial plan for profitability and need for new
capital

↓

Integrating the individual plans against the
financial plan for profitability and need for new
capital

↓

Integrating the individual plans with each other
and adjusting as necessary

↓

Working out action plans

↓

Budgeting

↓

Comparing plan with actual

↓

Modifying the strategy as necessary

↓

Working out new individual plans

1.12 KEYS TO GROWTH

Systematically seek out, find and reach for growth products and growth markets
Employ entrepreneurs to seek and promote new business opportunities

Be self critical about adequacy of the present operations thereby presenting superior competitive abilities

Top management should be composed of courageous, adventurous executives who are driven by an energetic zeal to lead but within financial guidelines

Establish formal systems of discovering opportunities and offsetting extreme risks through statements of company goals. Aim at creativity

Establish through the Chief Executive or Managing Director, an organisation environment of self-examination and effervescent high adventure

Accept that even through the cautious practicing of corporate planning, there is still no guarantee of success; bad decisions may not be eliminated but without planning it is still possible for companies to be successful, but not many

Corporate planning will fail where:
The Chief Executive or Managing Director does not believe in it and senior management commitment does not exist

The Chief Executive or Managing Director allows no-one but himself to make decisions

Time cannot be found to write down plans or develop the strategy

Company planner is not reporting directly to Chief Executive or Managing Director

There is no desire for better results than have been achieved without planning

Hasty declarations of company objectives

Lack of appreciation of value of planning

The company is sinking so fast that, in any case, planning doesn't matter

Return on Capital Pyramid

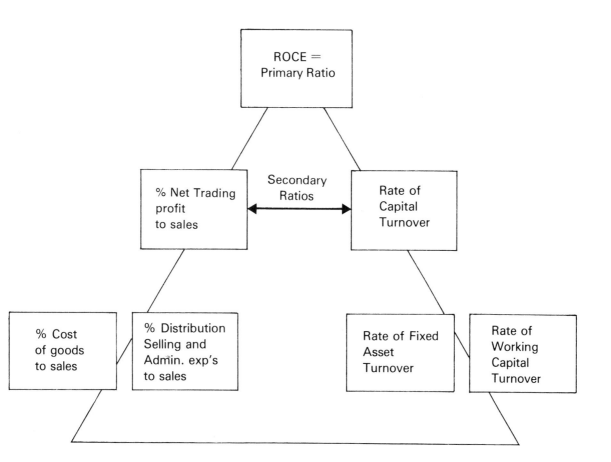

1.14 BUSINESS RELOCATION

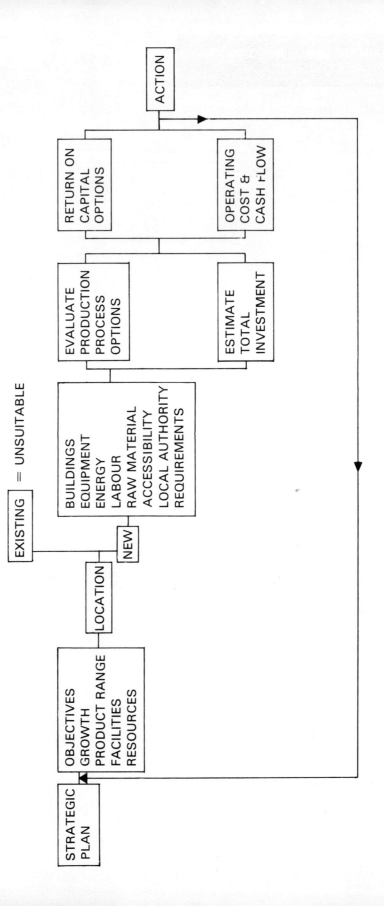

Business Relocation:

Government restrictions on development
Business growth
Shortage of labour
Technological change
Optimum size reached
Capital release

Investigate:

Sales forecasts
Labour costs
Labour availability
Equipment/construction facilities
Sites
Materials
Utilities
Government regulations
Financing

Note any decision must bear in mind:

Profitability
Expansion at existing locations
Manufacturing own products
Continuing in present type of business
Flexibility of proposed facilities
Future changes of processes, etc.
Location: Consider transportation as
proportion of total cost; the options
available, and over-dependence on
local supplies

Industrial Concentration:

Present company size
Remote and rural locations
Growth of business
Executive preference
Site availability
Labour availability

Advantages:

Proximity to market
Reduced transport costs
Availability of Labour
Prestige of location
Contact with customers and competitors
Contact with Government departments
Transport links
Educational facilities
Personal contacts with colleagues

Availability of specialist services, e.g. banking, insurance, maintenance services and
stocks of products

Disadvantages:

Lack of space
Premises difficult and costly to acquire
High staff turnover — scarcity and expense
of labour
Street and traffic congestion
Long journeys between home and workplace
Local competition
More militant labour force

When planning a move the following are necessary for success:

Proper co-ordination and control
Looking far enough ahead to the future
Not accepting status quo as basis
Business requirements — buildings, etc

Planning must include:

Sales forecasts
Product requirements
Make or buy analysis
Process layouts and flow process charts
Review of all production equipment and new
equipment requirements
Re-examination of machine capacities
Materials handling and stores requirements
Detailed factory layouts — some of the fac-
tors to be taken into account are:
The material flow pattern
The site
Routing of services
The need for flexibility
The production area
Personnel movement
Location of noisy dirty processes
Schedules of new and existing plant
Ordering and delivery dates of new equip-
ment
Maintenance requirements for plant and
buildings
Location of services requirements
Administrative organisation
Final plant layouts
Time schedules for the implementation of
the above
Building specifications

Disposal of plant and equipment at old location

The financial analysis of project involves a complete financial analysis not only during the initial decision but also during the planning. This must include capital expenditure and profit and loss projections

Use decision trees, discounted cash flow and risk analysis techniques for choosing courses of action, but the final decision will be partially subjective

Financial control regarding capital expenditure sanctions, revisions of capital and operating budgets and actual expenditure is essential

The main areas for Capital Budget Expenditure are:
> Land
> Buildings
> Equipment
> Transfer and start up expenses

Note also:
Revenue from existing premises and possible Government financial aid

Personnel:
> Tell employees as soon as possible about the relocation
> Negotiate with employee representatives and trade unions
> Use manpower planning to establish staffing levels
> Arrange redundancy/termination arrangements

> When selecting staff to be transferred to a new location, consider:
> The cost advantages of transferring
> The manpower availability at the new location
> Availability of housing and other facilities for staff moved
> Reaction of population at the new location to influx of newcomers
> Desirable to take jobs and not people to a Development Area
> Desirable to take people not jobs to a New Town

Assistance:
> No change of residence — reimburse travelling costs (period of 1 year) allow for extra travelling time adjust salary

Change of residence:
> Expenses paid visits to new area (employees and dependents)
> Liaison with local house agents
> Reimbursement of legal and professional fees
> Removal expenses paid
> Expenses paid house-hunting visits
> Disturbance allowance
> Interest free loans
> Travelling costs from temporary accommodation

Recruitment of new staff
> Organise facilities
> Set up interview stages

The Move:
> A sufficiently senior member of management must be appointed
> The location must be independent in terms of administration and self-government

Problems experienced:
> Design and construction deficiencies
> Delays in the provision of service facilities by the local town administration
> Numerous minor problems, e.g. lights, drainage, etc.
> Equipment necessary after the move
> Insufficient preparation of maintenance procedures
> The effectiveness and efficiency of the processing lines did not rise as fast as anticipated

General Points:
The majority of business can stand the disruptive effects of relocation. It may take quite some time for these to disappear and it will be the smaller firm that may not be able to stand these disruptions

In the main, there are few substantial costs savings to be made as a result of relocation

1.15 MANAGEMENT DO'S AND DON'TS

Don't sell what you haven't got

Don't take on more business than you can cope with

Don't take on work against another person's design without safeguards as to workability, design changes, price and delivery

Don't sell to a spectification you haven't achieved

Don't make 'specials' for which there is no general demand unless it is your business

Do ensure that product costs are realistic and reliable

Do introduce stable management policies

Do cut out loss making parts of the business and improve operations with low returns on capital employed

Do assume that there might be a better way of doing anything until the contrary is proved

Do remember that it is usually a relatively small amount of effort which produces most of the return

Do accept that often knowledge of what is being done is not as perfect as managers believe

Do recognise that the future is more important than the present

See Also

2 Management

Business is concerned with transactions in the market place and with supplying a service or buying, making and selling.

Business houses are like other systems and are capable of being analysed and synthesized.

To understand a business one must know

>   What is its overall purpose
>   How it is to be achieved
>   How to determine the most effective organisation of resources: people, money, raw materials
>   How to change its corporate strategy to meet changing market place needs

To run a business efficiently means to run it profitably with appropriate economic return on total capital invested: people, money and raw material

Long term and short term profits must be weighed against each other

There can be many individual businesses within a company usually referred to as a "Group"

Businesses within a company require to be appraised regularly covering the following problem areas:
>   Products and the customers' appraisal of them
>   Capability of the sales organisation
>   Production facilities and their technological status and economic viability
>   Development of the market with respect to the market size, the technical demands on the product, the structure of the customers, the sales channels and the competition
>   Capability of the business or company for adapting its product and its selling methods to the future demands of the market

Market planning and financial planning occupy a central position.

Centralised

v

Decentralised

Centralised

Advantages:

> Strong authority at the top where overall decisions are made because it is the meeting point of all information

> Easy recruitment of middle managers usually promoted from the ranks

Disadvantages:

> The whole firm depends on one man to grasp everything, and whose replacement becomes very difficult. He tends to become authoritative, refusing dialogue and delegation of authority

> The department managers are not able to make sophisticated decisions and to overcome their specialisation; neither are middle managers, whose promotion is difficult due to their lack of preparation in supervising activities

> Contacts between technical and marketing functions are made at the top and impede good comprehension of numerous techniques and diversified markets

> The whole system depends on command or negotiations. It prevents initiative and flexibility

Decentralised

Advantages:

> It frees top management from having to make short-term decisions

> It helps to fix accountability, spreads out responsibility, and motivates managers who

become responsible for their performance and can evaluate it

It is very flexible, permits handling diversified techniques and markets, for it brings the decision-making closer to the scene of action It fosters initiative

Disadvantages:

It requires capable managers

The decentralised unit may become so independent that it may actually begin to work against the interests of the company as a whole

The manager may maximise short-term gains at the expense of long-term goals.
He may show outstanding results for a time by not replacing tangible assets when he should, by overloading customers, or cutting down research

Decentralisation increases administrative expense, since many of the staff functions at headquarters have to be duplicated in the divisions if the division manager is to do the job properly

Top management must be strong for it is its responsibility to avoid these risks and control consistency between decentralised unit operations and corporate objectives

What kind of a structure does a business need to perform its job effectively?

What activities are necessary to achieve the purpose of the business?
What decisions will have to be made?
What relationships are necessary between the people forming the structure?

The attitude of the Chief Executive is crucial, one must:

help to set demanding corporate goals
reshape the organisation to fulfil the goals required;
encourage an awareness of change in all aspects of company environment
motivate cooperation, communication, collaboration and interdependence in all managerial roles
encourage the development of applicable corporate strategies
monitor the effectiveness of these strategies
develop suitable managerial incentives

Improvement of performance by providing means with which each manager can monitor and help improve his or her standard

Management by objectives requires certain basic steps on the part of management. Any MBO system must include:

reviewing critically and restating the company's strategic and tactical plans

clarifying with each manager his key results and performance standards and gaining his contribution and commitment to these — the relationship between each manager must be fully understood so that teamwork is facilitated

establishing rigorous procedures for control and self-control of progress — this will always include performance and potential review

establishing imaginative management development programmes, including training plans, selection, salary and succession plans

providing conditions in which these results can be achieved, this means a supportive climate of opinion, effective organisation structure and sound management control information

Problems encountered when applying MBO

distrust by employees
resentment by management
problems of management commitment to written assessment
need for management to set valid objectives
lack of data
need for top management backing

Implementation of Management by Objectives

Introduction to senior management — total involvement and acceptance required
Set Management Guides
a) results analysis
area under consideration
standard expected
standard achieved
b) job description
main purpose
position in organisation
size of job
limits of authority

Agree with managers
Set timescale for plan
Review performance

Measure of success

ratio of internal placements to external appointments
management standards rise with more professional approach
better organisation structures
more accountability within the structure
more emphasis on training for specfic performance improvement

Definition: **A Manager**

Needs no supervision

Is responsible for the functioning of his unit all the time, whether he is there or not

Writes, transmits and applies the rules for his unit

Does not allow an employee to occupy a post or undertake a task for which he is not trained

Delegates but does not abdicate

Knows his reputation is less important than that of the group

Ensures someone is responsible for every task at every moment

Looks at his unit through the customers eyes

Ensures his personnel concentrate on service even when they are very busy

Sets up a strong team to maintain standards of quality and service in his unit. The strength of his team determines his promotion prospects

Is interested in his staff members, and provides them with:
technical training
commercial motivation
the practice of responsibility

Must be investigative, adaptable, available

The Manager's role:

Set objectives and goals for each work area and to plan how to reach those goals

Organise work. To analyse, divide and allocate work to groups and individuals

Motivate and communicate. To create a team to provide incentives of the right kind and the information which people need

Measure results. To check against plans, see that each man knows what he is doing and where he fits in

Develop people — or to manage them in a way which enables them to develop themselves

Fundamental to the success for business is managing of managers. Management is the one function which operates only on people and in a wide variety of circumstances. Every manager, by and large, has under him people who manage other people.

The way in which managers are managed determines the level of performance of the management effort.

From the performance of the management effort stems the performance of the business or enterprise

A manager in managing subordinates must:

Ensure that the vision, wills and efforts of his subordinates are directed to the goals of the business, i.e. total commitment to laid-down objectives

Structure his subordinates jobs so that they are able to perform effectively, i.e. analyse, divide and allocate work to groups and individuals

Create the right spirit in which the team element can develop; to motivate and communicate and measure achievements

Take steps to develop his subordinates to provide tomorrows higher levels; help them to develop themselves

A manager develops through:

Sincere objective appraisal of performance

Financial rewards directly related to performance

Job satisfaction

A promotion system based on performance

Each job structured in such a way that the definition and limits are laid down e.g. division of work, authority and responsibility, discipline, unity of direction, stability, conditions and iniative are all pre-requisites to the measurement of performance

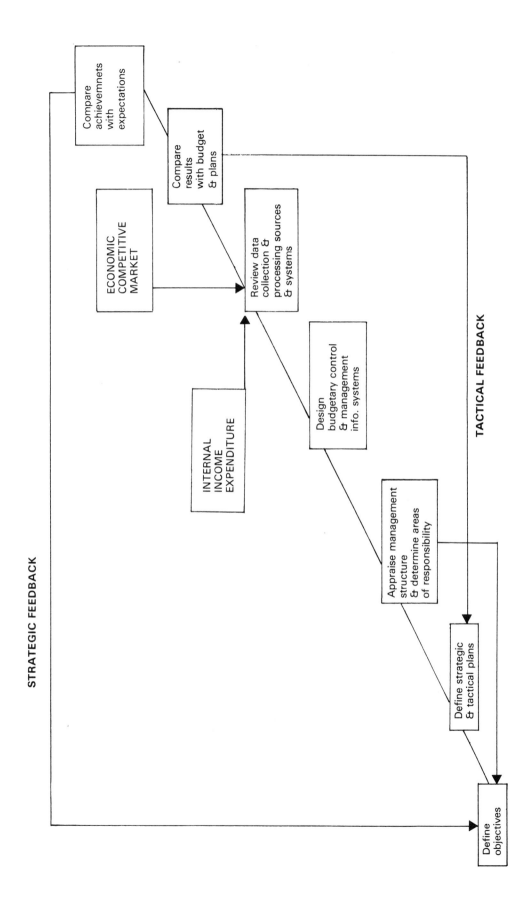

DATA CATCHMENT	DATA CONVERSION	DATA OUTPUT

DATA CATCHMENT

A. ENVIRONMENTAL
  Social
  Political
  Economic

B. COMPETITIVE
  Market Share
  Past Performance
  Present Activity
  Strategic Plans

C. ACCOUNTING
  Financial Accounting
  Management Accounting

DATA CONVERSION

```
F     M            M
I     A            A
N     N            N
A     A            A
N A   G            G A
C C ─► E S ─►       E C
I C ◄─ M T ◄─       M C
A O   E R          E O
L U   N U          N U
  N   T C          T N
  T   T            T
  I   U            I
  N   R            N
  G   E            G
```

DATA OUTPUT

PROFIT AND LOSS STATEMENTS
  Company
  Division
  Unit
  Department

NET ASSET STATEMENTS
  Company
  Division

CASH MOVEMENT

MANAGEMENT RATIOS

FORECASTS — SHORT TERM

Is information presented in such a way that it assists in decision-making?

Does information indicate each responsible individual's achievements and level of required performance? Are responsibilities clearly defined?

Does the information presented to him enable the individual manager to make plans and set standards?

Do reports present both results and — insofar as possible — the reasons behind these results?

Are past and present levels of performance emphasised in reports?

Is the reporting structure flexible?

Are established goals and other standards stressed as benchmarks in reports?

Is information about the future given in reports?

Is information of a non-financial nature reported where it has relevance to financial outcomes?

Is information on external conditions (as they might bear on a particular organisation's operations) given in reports?

Is each report oriented towards its recipient, considering both his level and function?

Do reports give as much information as possible in quantitative terms?

Are reports suitably succinct? Is exception reporting encouraged?

Are recipients of reports urged to consider fully their content and to discuss this with colleagues and staff?

Is an appropriate and known degree of accuracy secured in reported information?

Does management realise that the study of management information and reporting systems is not necessarily concerned with computers?

Is it understood that more data in reports does not in itself mean more information for management?

Does management know that information needs cannot all be predetermined by systems studies?

Is it appreciated that for information to be instantly available does not necessarily increase its value or usefulness? And that frequent reporting does not necessarily mean that information is thereby more useful? Half accurate information on time is better than totally correct information too late.

Is management by exception practised in designing and compiling reports?

Are reports understood?

Is unnecessary detail eliminated from reports?

Do reports call the attention of higher levels of management to those situations that cannot be controlled at lower levels?

Is each report that is produced really necessary?

Can reports be condensed, or combined one with another?

Can the frequency of issue of reports be altered?

Is an interest in the reporting system maintained at all levels of management?

Can significant figures be produced and communicated between normal reporting dates?

Are regular review meetings held to consider reports, results, and the adequacy of reporting systems?

Are attempts made to explain variations from plan in an upwards direction in the organisation before criticism proceeds downwards to the source of variation?

Are the duties and responsibilities of all those concerned with producing reports clearly defined?

Is the chart of accounts compatible with the requirements of the reporting system? Does either take precedence?

Are controllable expenses segregated from those that are non-controllable?

Are results reported in the same manner in which managers plan and think about their operations?

Are reports presented in an easy-to-read format?

Is appropriate use made of ratios and percentages?

Are figures in reports rounded whenever possible?

Is follow-up properly planned?

Can the reader grasp easily the developments from the reports, act on these or ensure other action?

2.9 NEW PROBLEMS FACING MANAGEMENT

New and flexible approaches to management thinking are required to meet a new social conscience within a framework of existing social and economic problems.

How much control should workers have?

What status should they have based on their social contribution?

What is the social value of the individual?

What are reasonable or good working conditions?

How much involvement should unions be offered?
Equal opportunities
Race relations

Should worker directors be appointed?

Should share/profit schemes be offered?

How does inflation affect the Unions?

Cash flow problems and erosion of the capital base with ever increasing cost spiral for raw material created by inflation

Increasing government participation requirements

Strength or vulnerability of the pound (or local currency) for imports and exports

Stop-go policy with regard to the availability and limit of credit from the Exchequer

Competition from Abroad

Hankering after decentralisation needs strong central policies

What kind of a structure does a business need to perform its job effectively?

What activities are necessary to achieve the purpose of the business?

What decisions will have to be taken?

What relationships are necessary between the people forming the structure?

Decision making process:

Define the problem

Locate the critical factor

Determine the conditions for its solution, the need to meet objectives and the balance between present and future

Analyse the problem

Find the facts necessary to a solution and capable of being obtained

Know where facts stop and assumptions begin

Develop alternative solutions; including 'do nothing'

Choose between solutions using as criteria for choice: risk, economy of effort, timing limitation of resources

Make the solution effective

Are individuals' responsibilities clearly defined?

Is the assigned authority in line with delegated responsibility in all cases?

Is delegation properly carried out?

Is the organisation chart current, adequately detailed, and available to all staff?

Could any organisational grouping be re-organised to reduce costs or improve effectiveness?

Are objectives — both corporate and departmental — established and communicated?

Are key assignments rotated? Should they be; and, if so, can they be?

Is management succession planned?

Are responsibilities divided in such a way as to permit a budgetary measurement of individual effectiveness?

Are all responsible individuals called upon to explain variances in their areas? Are follow-up actions checked?

Is every necessary function unambiguously assigned to a responsibility centre?

Are responsibilities specific and understood?

Is there any overlapping of responsibilities?

Does each individual within the organisation have one — and only one — boss?

Does an adequate coding system exist so that all cost items can readily be recorded in their proper account?

Does the chart of accounts accurately represent the organisational structure as it is rather than as it perhaps should be? Does the management information system reflect the structure?

Are all items of expense recorded in accordance with the lowest level or area of operations to which they can be directly related?

Are all needless allocations and apportionments avoided?

2.11 RESPONSIBILITY ACCOUNTING
(cont)

```
┌─────────────┐        ┌──────────────┐
│ Design      │───────▶│ Establish    │
│ management  │        │ areas of     │
│ structure   │        │ individual   │
│             │        │ responsibility│
└─────────────┘        └──────────────┘
                              │
                              ▼
        ┌──────────────┐          ┌──────────────┐
        │ Review       │          │ Define       │
        │ periodically │          │ control      │
        │ income &     │          │ criteria     │
        │ cost centres │          │ i.e. overhead│
        │ i.e. improve │          │ levels;      │
        │ income,      │          │ ratios etc.  │
        │ reduce costs │          │              │
        └──────────────┘          └──────────────┘
                    │          │
                    ▼          ▼
            ┌──────────────┐  ┌──────────────┐
            │ Review       │  │ Review over- │
            │ necessity    │  │ heads of each│
            │ of each      │  │ function or  │
            │ function or  │  │ cost centre  │
            │ cost centre  │  │              │
            └──────────────┘  └──────────────┘

┌──────────────┐  ┌──────────────┐  ┌──────────────┐
│ Establish    │  │ Establish    │  │ Reconcile    │
│ criteria     │  │ income       │  │ depart-      │
│ for new      │  │ cost budgets │  │ mental budgets│
│ functions    │  │ for each     │  │ with total   │
│              │  │ function     │  │ company      │
│              │  │              │  │ budget       │
└──────────────┘  └──────────────┘  └──────────────┘

┌──────────────┐  ┌──────────────┐  ┌──────────────┐
│ Analyse      │  │ Monitor &    │  │ Compare      │
│ income &     │  │ discuss      │  │ income &     │
│ cost         │  │ individual's │  │ costs with   │
│ variances.   │  │ perf-        │  │ budget       │
│ Agree changes│  │ ormance      │  │              │
│ where        │  │ against      │  │              │
│ necessary    │  │ appraisal    │  │              │
│              │  │ criteria     │  │              │
└──────────────┘  └──────────────┘  └──────────────┘
```

Are all changes in responsibilities made with a clear understanding of their impact on the part of all concerned?

Are all cases of promotion, salary increases, and disciplinary action approved by the immediate superior of the individual?

Do all disputes over questions relating to authority and responsibility receive prompt and careful consideration?

Are accurate standards set for each measurable and controllable cost element?

Are all costs clearly split into their controllable and uncontrollable categories (bearing in mind the level of authority and the time span)?

Is cost consciousness encouraged throughout the organisation?

Do cost controls correspond with areas of organisational responsibility?

Is the performance of each responsible individual regularly measured, monitored and reported?

Are the plans/standards used in performance measurement adequate and sufficiently accurate?

Discussion and arrangement of terms of transaction or agreement:
  Levels:
        person to person
        group to group
        organisation to organisation
        international negotiations
  Selection of committee:
        Is it representative?
        Has it status and authority for credibility?
        Do not include senior management
        Include members who will administer agreement
        Include younger members to gain experience
  Information useful to committee:
        Age, length service etc.
        Personal connection and concerns
        General details (hobbies etc.)
        Reasons why on committee
  General:
        Use visual aids, e.g. graphs etc.
        Direct attention towards quantifiable numbers
        Preparation requires discipline
        Humour is a valuable aid and its use can be encouraged
        Allocate issues to members according to individual credibility,
        Allocate responsibility for taking notes during meeting
        Write agenda
  Impasse:
        Have all possible information, positions, compromises, evaluations and emotions been extracted from the discussion?
        What are the possibilities of reaching tentative agreement on the issue?
        Are there other issues which should be resolved before reaching tentative agreement on this one?
        What are the implications of being the party that recommends passing it for the present?
        Will further discussion only serve to further harden existing positions and threaten agreement on other issues?

Specific Uses:

    Current planning
    Long-term planning
    Testing potential
    Research & Development
    Capital investment
    Cash flow
    Financing (short and long-term)
    Manpower
    Distribution
    Production
    Raw materials
    Selling

Problems in Forecasting:

    Unrecognisable patterns
    Non-comparable situations
    New factors
    Slow changes
    Cycles: econometric
            seasonal

To help overcome these problems select the approach noting:

    What will the forecast be used for?
    What risks are there in the forecast?
    What is the forecast time scale?
    What period of historical data is available?
    What information is there available on similar activities?
    What accuracy is required?
    What time is available to prepare?
    What revisions will be possible?

Approach to forecasting:
    Statistical Analysis
    Subjective Judgement

Design Shortcomings:

    Bad location and design of service areas
    Inflexible design
    Physical conditions (e.g. noise, light etc.)
    Faults (e.g. slippery floors etc.)
    Maintenance (e.g. high cost and difficulty in cleaning)
    Large proportion of unusable space (e.g. stairs, corridors etc.)

To avoid these faults:

    set up small project team (possible varying composition during project)
    give team a closely involved chairman

Budgets must:

specify require-ments	state flexibility
	give cost analysis
state location	discuss finance

Types of building contract:
    tendering
    negotiation
    'Package'

Technical problems:

noise	site composition
smell	size
dust	shape
daylight	drainage

Office environment:

illumination level	noise levels
daylight	space
colour	communications
design	telephone, mail
temperature	flexibility
draughts	office machinery
humidity	filing
rate of change of air	general storage

Note: For every new building a booklet should be produced for all staff, showing the layout, services

Applications:

to present facts, concepts and information in a structured and effective form

to create positive attitudes, or correct negative ones, towards, an industry, product, service, concept

to create new opportunities to reach specific individuals or groups

to gain attention (at exhibition, trade shows etc)

to motivate their audiences towards a positive decision

Situations of Use — direct promotion of a product or service via:

invited customer gatherings

face to face presentations on desk top projectors to individual customers

planned non-theatrical library distribution:

point of sale promotions in retail outlets

public relations activities, particularly for general marketing development purposes

internal information e.g. induction

new product launches

internal sales training

retailer/dealer sales training and information servicing training, and as a form of service manual particularly for dealers

product information programmes (up-dating information)

exhibitions and trade shows:

direct promotion to the specific market sectors

Briefing of Audio Visual Team:

role in the total marketing communications context

audience attitudes to be created

who precisely are the groups and individuals that need to be reached?

what are their existing attitudes to and preknowledge of the programme subject?

which audio-visual distribution media is most suitable?

what communication opportunities can be created in which the audio-visual message can be presented to intended audiences?

in what environment(s) will the audience(s) receive the message? office, exhibition, hotel etc?

what support is required from other media? — brochures, handbooks

the cost parameters which the production and distribution objectives entail

Remember that an audio-visual aid helps a poor speaker

it is a 'normal' and expected medium to use at a presentation

retention is aided by the production of leaflets, brochures etc., for people to take away

use the full range of effects available with each audio-visual medium because the audience expects professionalism

a professional, practical presentation is always needed with audio-visual aids for speaking

the audio-visual aid can never do the whole job — needs the help of the presenter to set the scene

2.16 TYPES OF AUDIO VISUAL AID MEDIA

16mm film:

    flexible
    range of effects
    expensive
    long production time
    difficult to change or update
    needs external production
    widely used
    good quality large picture
    poor daylight viewing
    distribution outlets available

Slide with Audio Tape:

    easy to incorporate amendments
    multi image/screen effects
    simple to have different versions of one
    programme
    can be produced in house
    slides easy to obtain
    good impact
    adaptable for small/large gatherings

Video:

    easy to use
    'normal' medium view
    heavy, non mobile equipment
    incompatibility between makes
    limited audience size
    quick to produce
    no good for fine detail
    primarily "studio" based
    immediate replay

Overheard projector slides:

    cheap
    poor quality
    unsuitable for large audience

Flip Charts:

    very cheap
    difficult to read
    easily damaged

2.17 INDUSTRIAL MANAGEMENT PROBLEMS

Achieving partnership between Government and business in public service while preserving competitive outlook — retention of virtues of both systems

Becoming trusted by Government as public servants accountable to them — given delegated responsibility and authority and bringing about withdrawal of Governments from detailed restraints and interference with industry

Obtaining willing acceptance of planned economy and mixed economy by business and by Government

Development, management and direction of foreign affiliates, with appropriate degrees of private or public national participation in ownership and/or management

Age and succession. Retiring age and longevity

Adjusting industry to democratic tendencies — questions of centralisation and decentralisation

Size and scale

Efficiency and productivity and of permitted degrees of co-operation

Finance — take-overs, mergers, retained profits

Engineering — of development and applied science, as contrasted with pure science, physics and chemistry

Paternalism, associated with growth and remoteness, and problems of human sensitivity sufficient to pioneer and anticipate

Inevitability of technology and the need to harness it

Financial resources in ever expanding economies, and of foreign currency needs

Commercial and investment policies

Redundancies and technical progress

Weighing up world-wide excessive demand against pressures for shorter hours and less work

Advertising and selling, including restraints to damp down inflationary spending

Personal responsibilites of community leadership for industrial leaders — local or national

Education and training right up to senior management, with emphasis on recruitment, training and promotion of potential leaders

Early selection of future leaders

Acquiring mentality to welcome unsuspected future changes as well as past

Communications upwards and downwards inwards and outwards

Personality, of touch

Distribution — poverty amid plenty

Spreading the best management technique round the world

How to make the manager with a specialist skill into a leader able to take quick decisions over a wider front

How to prevent large businesses becoming too departmental and too full of specialists

See Also:

3 Marketing and Selling

3.1 FORMULATION OF MARKETING PLAN

Research work needed

General:

How does marketing research expenditure compare with competitors?
What marketing research has been accomplished in home and export markets?
How effective was it?
Has the firm efficient information sources?
What data is there available?
What methods of marketing research have been found to be effective?
What experimentation is taking place?
Are independent agencies preferred to firms own research?
How can product intelligence be obtained?

Market:

total size of market
rate of change of size
factors affecting changes
number of competitors
competitors' market share
competitors' change in market share
competitors' sales organisation structure
ruling current market prices
forecasts of market conditions
seasonal/cyclical market fluctuations
market potential (new and existing)
user characteristics/attitudes/opinions
potential customers — kind, number and location
product uses
customers' product selection criteria (e.g. performance size, shape, service
sources of customer dissatisfaction
competitive position of company products
distribution methods

3.2 INFORMATION REQUIRED FOR MARKETING PLAN

Economic:

industry cycles	lead time for deliveries
profits	unemployment
share prices	production
gross national product	gross domestic product
order/sales cycle	profit cycle & trends
investment cycle	trends of activity (growth/decline)

Political:
Price Commission or similar body
regional development legislation policies
monopolies and office of Fair Trading rules
wage restraint

Social and Environmental Legislation:

pollution	working
lighting	heating
ventilation	noise
legislation	scarce resources
pressure for recycling of natural resources	

Competitors' Activities:

competition's strengths and weaknesses in pricing policy
attitude to fixed price contracts and escalation
pricing policies — flexible prices reigning
servicing policy
type of distribution/selling cover
promotion activity/mail shots/product catalogues/operators and services manuals
policy to debtors/creditors leasing
patents restricting market
substitute product evaluation
market outlet — degree sophistication
level service required
potential purchasing power total market
strength/weaknesses product within market
growth/decline of market

Sampling:

Cheaper and quicker than a 100 per cent survey.

A higher quality survey because of a smaller sample size.

Sample size depends on degree of precision, but allow for non-response.

Accuracy and power of the forecast required

Use past to estimate the future but gauge importance

Terms of Reference:

information required
timescale
budget
sources available
scope of survey
decisions to be made from survey

Conducting the Survey

Questionnaire design:

unstructured — uses only interview guide
impossible to analyse
useful for formulating and checking ideas
can omit significant questions
and encourage irrelevancies
semi-structured — standard questions cope
with most responses
ease of tabulation/analysis
ease of recording
questionnaire covers all points required
needs to be designed well
structured questionnaire
only for very simple information

Note: design questionnaire with:

space for easy recording answers
stimulating and orientating early questions
important questions early on

Method of Contact

Requirements of method chosen:

collect information speedily
produce information cheaply
cope with large volumes of information
generate quantitive information
produce new ideas
ask complex questions
probe in depth
give due weight to expert informants
protect against bias
check validity of the answers
explain divergence of opinions
ensure anonymity/confidentiality of
individual opinions

Personal interview:

expensive
slow (1 hour per person)
answers can be checked
probing/follow up questions

Telephone interview:

speed
lower cost
small volumes of information
no complex questions
avoid being nuisance
difficult to check answers
difficult to establish rapport
relieves salesmen of routine tasks

Postal questionnaire:

low cost
low unpredictable response rate (5 to 10 per cent)
follow-up mailings
can provide blanket coverage
no interview control
sensitive information will not be given
only a few questions to be asked

Group Discussions:

need six to ten people

3.4 MARKETING PLAN RESOURCE ALLOCATION

A Marketing orientated company places customers and their needs at centre of business

Marketing:

> fits a business to its customers' needs
> seeks to achieve more effective selling by looking ahead
> optimum profit from minimum cost
> aims to give direction and purpose to management

Resource allocations depend on:

> today's and tomorrow's winners
> productive specialities
> development products
> failures and their corrections
> repair jobs
> unnecessary specialities
> unjustified specialities
> investments in managerial ego

Allocation of key resources should be mainly to those products which will show worthwhile results

Today's winners are at or close to their peak and any excessive allocation of resources to them should be cut back

Results are obtained by exploiting opportunities not by solving problems alone

3.5 MARKETING DEPARTMENT ORGANISATION

From these produce systematic list of tasks for next 12 months in marketing department

What is required to know and be able to do tasks?

Should use be made of:

> External courses
> 'Tailored' courses (external)
> Internal courses
> Instruction and guided self development

Organisation

3 Key areas:
> Sales
> Product development
> New products

Training — identifying needs:
Marketing plan
> Department objectives
> Job descriptions

Personnel:

Consider the following:
> Basic training
> Job history
> Qualifications required
> Working relations required
> Functional relations required

3.5 MARKETING DEPARTMENT ORGANISATION (cont)

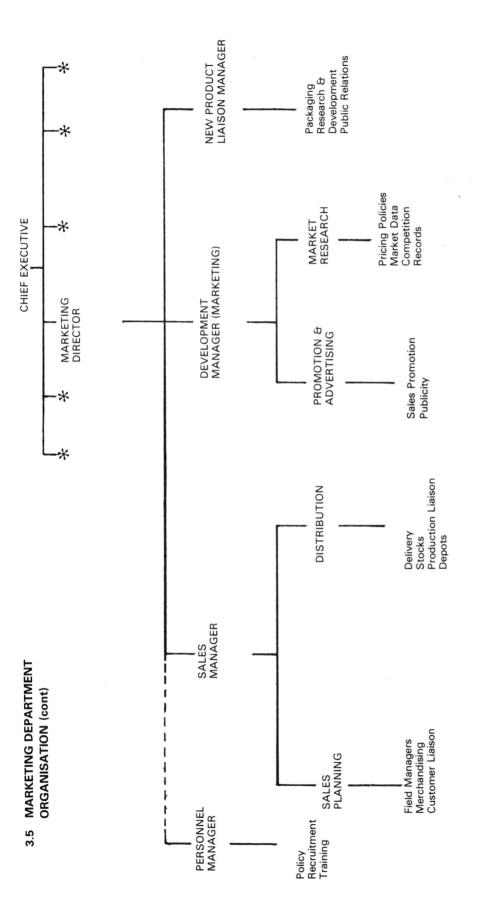

CHIEF EXECUTIVE

MARKETING DIRECTOR

PERSONNEL MANAGER
- Policy
- Recruitment
- Training

SALES MANAGER

SALES PLANNING
- Field Managers
- Merchandising
- Customer Liaison

DISTRIBUTION
- Delivery
- Stocks
- Production Liaison
- Depots

DEVELOPMENT MANAGER (MARKETING)

PROMOTION & ADVERTISING
- Sales Promotion
- Publicity

MARKET RESEARCH
- Pricing Policies
- Market Data
- Competition
- Records

NEW PRODUCT LIAISON MANAGER
- Packaging
- Research & Development
- Public Relations

New products:

What market share can be expected if company continues on its present course?
How will customer requirements and habits change?
What new markets are suitable?
What will be their sales potential?
When will this potential be reached?
What will need to be done — development; production; sales?
What resources will be needed e.g. manpower?
Will financial resources be sufficient?
Will specialists be needed?
What will be the profit margin?
Can an adequate market share be obtained?
How fast will the market grow?
How is the demand divided — Government/industrial/military/private export?
What future market share can be expected if products are modernised?
How will sales increase if the product range is extended?
Can the sales effort be intensified and what effect will this have?

Market changes:

How will customers' demands affect product?
How will composition of customers change?
What will happen to price levels?
What government action may happen?
How will sales channels alter e.g. franchising?
Are there any cyclical changes within the industry?
Will energy prices e.g. oil or gas affect demand?
Can industrial action offset supply of raw material e.g. national coal strike?

Are product markets mature or growing?
How strong against competition is the product range of company X?
Are competitors likely to become more effective in the near future?
Are the markets for the products of company X growing or declining? How and why?
Will company X still be successful for the foreseeable future?

Stages in product acquisition:
exploration
screening
investigation
proposition
negotiation
integration

Key pitfalls:

Not placing responsibility at a sufficiently high level
Failing to establish a real unanimity of opinion as to what the acquisition objectives should be
Setting unrealistic criteria for to-day's competitive sellers' market
Searching only among companies for sale
Failing to recognise the time required for a successful acquisition programme
Failing to focus the search correctly
Failing to investigate prior to actual negotiations
Failing to assess correctly a seller's motives
Overlooking opportunities by using mechanical screening procedures
Failure to obtain qualified outside assistance when needed
Too much analysis and too little action, or vice-versa

Success criteria:

To establish clearly defined growth objectives
Sound internal organisation to establish acquisition criteria

3.8 MANAGEMENT REQUIREMENTS FOR NEW PRODUCT PLANNING

Business strategy is expressed in products. Product programmes are the foundation of forward company planning

The new product programme is a top management responsibility

The new product function should be organised as a top executive staff function, headed by a person who can work effectively at top management level with accountability

Organisation and control should be established in conformance with the stages of new product evolution:

exploration

↓

screening

↓

business analysis

↓

development

↓

testing

↓

commercialisation

New products require co-ordinated effort which is best achieved through interdepartmental product teams, representing all functional areas of the business; tailored to fit the characteristics of each product

A definite programme, carefully planned and closely managed, significantly improves new product results

New idea creation can be directed and controlled to achieve improved pertinence and quality of product ideas

New product selection is accomplished by a continuing series of evaluation at all stages. No single screening is adequate

Selection standards for products to be developed should be upgraded persistently to achieve an ever-increasing yield from available manpower and resources

Product planning requires adequate specifications and a programme for each product prior to laboratory development

Market requirements and opportunities are the primary consideration in product planning

Company acquisition should be integrated with internal development to achieve a balanced new product programme.

3.9 NEW PRODUCT PLANNING STAGES

Screening:

    expand idea into a full product concept
    collect facts and opinions
    appraise idea for potential value
    test opinion
    produce written report

Business analysis:

    appoint production team for further study of idea
    determine feasibility of large scale production
    develop specifications and establish a definite programme for the product
    do preliminary market research
    set up timetable for product launch

Development:

    establish development projects for each product
    build product to designated or revised specifications
    complete laboratory evaluation and release for testing
    continue market research

Testing:

    plan commercial experiments necessary to test and verify earlier judgments of the product
    conduct in-use, production, and market testing
    make final product decision, freeze design

Commercialisation:

    complete final plans for production and marketing
    initiate co-ordinated production and selling programmes
    check results — make necessary improvements in product, manufacturing, or sales
    monitor design faults

3.10 DIRECT MAIL, ADVERTISING AGENCIES

Direct Mail

Mail sent to specific addresses for advertising prepared the way for the sales force and can act in these ways:

    advertising — influencing attitudes
    sales promotion — obtaining leads
    direct selling — obtaining sales

Advantages:

    selectivity
    personal approach
    nearly always looked at
    variety of formats
    flexibility
    reply paid response cards

    Note: bulk rebate system from the Post Office

Assessment of success:

    cost per reply
    number read by customers (from representatives' sales reports)

Advertising agencies

Because techniques are becoming increasingly complex and elaborate, the use of an agency is compelled to maintain quality

Research work should be independent from advertising agency:

    agencies do not generally have comprehensive research department
    possible bias within agency between creative and research sides

3.11 ADVERTISING CHECK LIST ON USE

Types of media:

newspapers
trade papers
television
radio
cinema
subscription journals
business supplements
posters
placards
direct mail
exhibitions
educational campaigns
export journals
institute publications
other publications

Reason for use:

changes opinions and attitudes — level of change depends on frequency and quality

market share depends on opinions of product

significantly improves level of sales closings (especially where no regular customer contact)

reduces costs of selling — if adequate frequency

advertising in well advertised market increases cost of selling

Allocation of funds:

existing production capacity
saturation point where resources become limited or expensive
rate of market response to extra sales and marketing effort
future market growth potential
use contribution figures after direct costs instead of sales figures
use true gross profit to net profit monetary values instead of % figures (relieves the considerable confusion created thereby)
cost product groups down to net profit contribution (show marketing support costs in each group)

Media strategy:

Is the market horizontal (everybody) or vertical (selective)?

Where the primary objective of a press campaign is to enhance the reputation of the advertiser, large spaces in horizontal media are most likely to succeed.

When the primary objective is enquiries, small spaces in vertical media are usually more appropriate, particularly where a reader reply service is operated by the publisher

Where the application of the product has distinct operational benefits, case-histories are often most effective

Where advantages are in the price/delivery/quality areas, a generalised customer-benefit approach is appropriate

Measuring effectiveness:

Aim:
to make advertising work harder and more effectively
to use professional and creative people
Do not:
assume you know your present and potential customers
use a publication or programme just because you like it
approach advertising with preconceived ideas
produce advertising that just pleases your boss
forget it is the effects of advertising that are most important — these must be measured

3.12 PUBLIC RELATIONS

Techniques:

> press releases
> handouts
> receptions and conferences
> open days
> facility and informal visits
> shareholders' meetings
> prestige films
> corporate status adveritising
> radio and TV participation in programmes
> sponsorship

Types of press release:

> case histories
> unusual product uses
> company magazines/brochures
> contract/order announcements
> sales milestones
> continuity of supply
> quality control
> after-sales service
> factory/plant development
> research activities
> policy changes
> marketing changes
> special promotions
> new staff appointments
> first/large/unusual export order
> record output
> participation in overseas trade exhibitions

Factors for new/modified product announcements:

> description
> cost
> availability
> applications
> prospective purchasers
> competitors' product comparison
> sales offices addresses
> dealer details
> promotions available
> research details
> outline other new products
> photographs

3.13 SALES — FACTORS INFLUENCING MARKET SHARE

Customer loyalty:

> how many suppliers to customer?
> how long have they been?
> rate of change of suppliers?
> rate of change of business between suppliers?
> how easy is it to change?

Suppliers' image:

Product attributes	Suppliers' attributes
quality	reliable delivery
performance	quick delivery
reliability	technical service
appearance	and advice
price	attention to complaints
ease of maintenance	order handling
full range	credit terms
	discounts
	commercial services

Competition activity:

> increasing/decreasing
> product comparison
> pricing
> availability

Market share ratios:

> cost per £x sales
> cost per customer serviced
> cost per sales transaction
> cost per £x gross contribution
> average selling cost per unit
> selling prices
> discount structures
> relative sales mixes
> gross/net contribution per representative
> gross/net contribution per sales area
> gross/net contribution per distribution area
> gross/net contribution per order
> administration costs (sales)

3.14 SALES FORCE STANDARDS OF PERFORMANCE

Is ratio of contracts/orders received to quotations submitted:

> increasing?
> static?
> decreasing?

Do we qualify needs and degree of interest of enquirer?

Do we establish:

> whether quotation is for future reference?
> whether purchase depends upon other negotiations?
> a firm intent to purchase?
> when completion/delivery is required?
> competitive involvement?
> maximum price?
> clear understanding of requirements?
> probability of successful negotiations?
> a provisional estimate prior to full quote?

Define size and type of quotation which should not require executive involvement

Institute a standard follow-up procedure — by correspondence/telephone

Submit reports of progress towards completion of negotiations

Quotations:

> Does the layout and general appearance of our quotations compare favourably with that of our competitors?
> For certain low-priced quotations, consider image, may appear too expensive to the customer?
> Are any people singularly successful in converting quotations into firm orders —
> if so, analyse methods used
> in the event of a contract or order being lost, obtain the true reason for failure
> indicate Conditions of Sale on every written quotation
> Endeavour to make 'on site' quotations for low-cost work and seek additional work at same time

3.15 CALL REPORTS

Completion of reports:

Do not waste management time by writing superfluous and unusable information, but do transmit essential information for prompt action

Reports from salesmen can show:

> value of sales
> number of sales
> category of sale
> sales target per period
> attainment towards target
> number of calls made
> number of new prospects found
> reason for no sale
> length of each interview
> quality of prospect
> number and date of return calls
> new accounts opened
> name and address of all calls
> complaints
> enquiries
> request for quotations
> progress on enquiries/quotations
> competitive activity

Analysis of Reports:

Use reports and records of salesmen to reveal average:
> call rate
> length of interview
> percentage of travelling time
> value of orders
> number of enquiries passed from head office
> conversion ratio of orders to enquiries

Are sales territory boundaries clearly defined?
Are maps of sales territories issued to salesmen?
Calculate the 'new business' potential in possible expanding areas
Are sales territories in line with possible increase of salesmen?

Why were you selling to the person in the first place?

How did you find the customer?

Was the customer a buyer for what you sell?

Did you quote because he really had a need, or because he wanted to shut you up?

What evidence had you that the customer had the money available to buy now?

Had he dealt with a competitor before?

Who got the order that time?

Had a competitor something the customer needed and you had not — or did not find out about?

Were you just a check on market price?

If so, why couldn't you show the customer more benefits in dealing with you?

Did you just quote for what the customer asked for, or what you found out he needed?

What feedback did you get from all the staff you spoke to during the survey?

As you went over the details with the customer, did you listen to what he was saying?

When your written proposition went in, did it show the benefits to the customer of the equipment, or just the specification and price?

Did you get the right method of acquisition — purchase, rental, hire purchase, leasing?

Did you let the customer get cold and miss out on follow up?

Would you have bought the scheme yourself, if you'd been the customer?

Was there conflict on design or anything else between you and the prospect of your own staff, that was pushed to one side or stamped on rather than resolved?

Could you genuinely answer every objection he raised?

Did you prove the answers?

Did you ask him why he did not buy?

Selling Process:

Sales representative introduces
self to new potential client

↓

Ask questions which identifies
clients needs and problems

↓

Translate problems into possible
profitable services

↓

Locate decision makers and
others in the decision making unit

↓

Adapt sales approach to different
interests of key executives

↓

Always identifies appropriate
stage of decision process

↓

Describe service feature
in terms of customer benefits

↓

Encourage a 'creeping commitment'
from the client

3.17 RECRUITMENT

Write job description:

    job title
    job holder
    reports to
    date
    job location
    authorities
    responsibilities
    staff reporting

Recruit:

    existing staff
    recommendations
    advertisements
    consultants
    head hunters
    local radio

Answering applicants:

    reject unsuitable
    check references — telephone
                       letter

Offer letter:

    salary
    hours of work
    enclose contract of employment
    holiday arrangements

Interview:

    psychological tests
    work history
    education
    family
    domestic situation
    financial situation
    health
    reasons for leaving

Making final choice rate candidates as follows:

    meets requirements — recommend
    better than average
    marginal
    poor — reject

3.18 SALES CALLS

Plan your sales calls ahead — at least one week

Distribute planned sales calls to colleagues

Spread type of calls — surveys, demonstrations and follow up quotations — evenly through the week

Keep up-to-date records on all customers

Do you know:

    proper name of company?
    affiliations in a group?
    credit rating?
    name of executive level contact?
    type of business?
    number of employees?
    have you ever made a survey or presented a proposal?
    if so for what application?
    is there any competitive equipment in use?
    if so for what application?
    for what area of use do you want your equipment considered?
    what items will you use to give backing to your case?
    what are the benefits your equipment offers this prospect?
    what experience stories of similar instllations will you use?
    have you sufficient examples, illustrations etc?
    what objections do you anticipate?
    have you at least one logical answer to each anticipated objection?
    what will you leave with the prospect to stimulate interest after you have gone?

Use the call reports to prepare accurate sales forecasts covering the next three months by establishing:

    which customers will make repeat orders?
    how much business will come from each customer?
    how many calls will be made during the period?
    performance ratios and average order values?

Selling can be broken down into two main headings — Product Knowledge and Selling Techniques

Product knowledge — the knowledge
>   what is/are the product/s?
>   what it does, how it works: benefits to the customer?
>   where can it be applied?
>   who is likely to buy it?
>   what is the vendor's sales policy?
>   how much does it cost, what are the margins?
>   what is the competition?

Selling techniques — the skill
>   territory planning:
>>   calculating and balancing workload
>>   plotting the customers
>>   segmenting the territory
>>   preparing and using a journey plan

>   how industries buy:
>>   who buys?
>>   when?
>>   why?
>>   how?
>   characteristics of the markets:
>>   prospecting
>>   researching
>>   telephoning
>>   cold calling
>   preparing for and starting the sales interview:
>>   identifying the customer's needs
>>   using questions
>>   selling benefits
>>   dealing with objections
>>   closing the sale
>>   using sales aids
>>   presentation techniques
>>   record-keeping procedures
>>   feeding back marketing information

This should give information:

>   about product
>   relevant to customer
>   about satisfied customers
>   utilise experienced professional help
>   at very beginning

Catalogues:
>   can they be combined from data sheets?

Sales publications — define the following:

>   who are we talking to?
>   what do we want to achieve?
>   what evidence do we already have?
>   what new facts/opinions do we have?
>   what objective evidence can we offer?

Prestige publications:

>   must avoid introversion and self-congratulation

Production of literature:

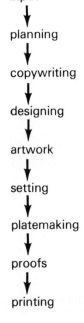

input

↓

planning

↓

copywriting

↓

designing

↓

artwork

↓

setting

↓

platemaking

↓

proofs

↓

printing

Note: for international literature there is a language problem and if it is very technical do not attempt to translate

3.21 SALES PROMOTIONS

Sales promotion should concentrate intensively on target groups already influenced by advertising:

    information
    consultation
    stimulation
    sales aids

Trade:

    incentives
    discounts
    free gifts
    competitions
    free offers

Consumer:

    discounts
    2 for the price of 1
    branded packs
    offers
    coupons
    special demonstrations
    free samples
    point of sale

Industrial:

    demonstrations
    exhibitions
    catalogues
    price lists
    technical leaflets
    display units
    'trade in' terms
    free gifts

3.22 IMPROVING PROFITABILITY AND PRODUCTIVITY

Short term

Evaluate products
↓
Detailed appraisal
↓
Set pricing policy
↓
Consider the discount policy
↓
Combat price competition
by raising or lowering prices

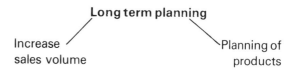

Long term planning

Increase sales volume   Planning of products

Effect of product mix on profits:

A company can make no more profit than its maximised product mix will allow

The practical criteria for evaluating products have reference to:

    market share
    the relevance of each product to the rest of the range
    the sales volume of the product
    the degree to which capital or other scarce resources are committed to the product, such as management or machine time
    the importance of the product to customers
    its vulnerability, in terms of markets, supplies or costs, to the impact of inflation or government or labour action
    sales forecasting/production planning, difficulties, short runs, etc
    its influence on credit, customer discounts or bad debts
    its impact upon company reputation
    the growth prospects in the market
    its coverage of overhead

the degree to which it ties up sales or service time
its impact upon costs such as waste, breakage, sales commissions
its market acceptance
market competition

These questions will lead to other more detailed appraisals:

How much could be gained by product modification or value analysis?

How far can the price be increased dramatically or the product quality be degraded, or both, either as a prelude to abandonment or in place of it?

How much could be gained by modifying the marketing and sales strategy?

How good are the alternative opportunities in this product area?

How much useful management time and resource can be gained by dropping the product?

How much in total monetary revenue is the product contributing beyond its direct costs, minus any indirect costs which are incurred marketing, selling and distributing this product specifically?

How much is the sale of this product contributing to the sale of other products in this range?

Has the market got potential for the future and, if so, what?

Long term planning of products and mix:

For long term planning purposes the following questions need to be asked:

When is the company likely to face situations of product shortage either because of materials supply or the disruption of production? How extensive are the situations likely to be?

How will competition attempt to reduce total demand, how do they allocate scarce products and how can the company gain a competitive or profitable advantage from this?

What role is played by sales management in deciding how such situations should be handled, and is the special difficulty of the personal selling task at this time recognised?

What are the implications of government policy and special legislation which may be prompted by company policies and which would damage either the market, the supply or long term company profitability?

Increasing sales volume:

cutting the size of the sales force
changing sales methods
improving volume per order
increasing the order to call ratio
increasing price, reducing discounts
lowering customer service levels
concentration upon high-growth, high-profit customers
area expansion
reduction of customer population
change of sales force remuneration, incentives
identifying marginal opportunities for growth
improving sales skills, product, or customer knowledge
key account development
providing sales and customer incentives

Product planning is essential, principles of which are:

To thoroughly measure the likely impact of inflation upon all key markets and products, and to pay close day to day attention to sudden developments

If the operation has to be cut back, cut it back hard though not necessarily fast, but do it earlier rather than later

Offer a tighter, streamlined product range with contingency funds held to exploit sudden opportunities

Develop overseas and other markets which are less prone to inflationary impact. To move from a high fixed cost manufacturing base towards a low fixed cost service organisation is one such option. Service organisations with low capital intensity seem to ride inflation rather better than manufacturing organisations

For new product development, speculate a little, particularly into those areas which do not tie up capital or technical resources and where there is a possibility of a small but fast payback. There are many such opportunities in the market which large companies often ignore because of their small potential size. These become much more attractive in times of zero growth. An acquisition policy towards innovative but small companies may be one answer

Invest at the point when the market is at its most depressed, when some are saying it will become even worse but the company judges it is improving. A high market share, established at the point when the market is depressed, will pay for itself handsomely when substantial volume reappears

Pricing policy:

A pricing policy must take into account a company's freedom to act within the following framework:

dominance of the company's market position
the degree to which substitute products are available
the likelihood of competitive response
the anticipated rise in costs
the degree to which sales and price are related within the chosen market sector
the company's long term business and market objective
the anticipated developments in technology
the need for company growth in sales volume
government restrictions on price
the company's short term profit requirement
relatively small pricing moves which may have a dramatic impact upon profits

Discount policy:

Alongside a sound pricing policy must be a valid and effective discount policy with adequate controls, since:

discounts may fall within pricing regulations
it is harder to reduce a customer's discounts than increase the list price
buyers seek more favourable discount terms when prices go up and play off one supplier against another
additional discounts tends to stay in the customer's pocket rather than being passed through to the end user, hence the market size is not increased
short term and promotional discounts have a tendency to become firmly established as standard discount
standard discounts for bulk orders or for rapid payments or for turnover volume have a tendency to be claimed, even when the conditions under which they are offered are not met

Criteria for combating price competition:

a lower price, and make a charge for delivery or for after sales service
lower prices for bulk orders delivered less frequently
lower prices against guaranteed orders over a period, paid in advance, or in stages
lower prices for sole supplier rights
reciprocal deals, with products and services being exchanged

Guidelines for altering product or service prices

Upwards:
Raise prices when everyone else does
Avoid too frequent price rises
Provide a short moratorium on the price increase for key customers
Provide advance notice of the price increase allowing customers to stock up at old prices
Offer some economy at the same time — a price reduction on small selling items — a promotional short term discount, and so on
Make a good case for the price increase, e.g. cost increases the lift in price, and also demonstrate how the company's productivity or profit improvement programme has

helped to absorb some of the increase

Show customers how they can change their buying pattern to minimise the effect of the increase

Introduce a new lower price, lower quality version of the product

Offer alternative payment or service terms

Downwards:

Cut the price when the competition is quiet, or preferably when they are raising their prices

Make the price cut deep enough. It has to be deep enough to overcome the normal inertia of the market and to 'pay' a buyer for his trouble in considering a new supplier

Do it without notice and promote it very widely. Be careful not to stock load large customers before-hand

Do it only when the price cut can be sustained for a long time, preferably when competition will have great difficulty in meeting it

Never do it unless the market is demonstrably price sensitive

Never do it as a crisis measure when profits are low and the market is turning down, competitors will copy to survive, and a price or discount war will result

Do it on selected loss leading lines, with other products trailed at normal prices

Cost control exists to ensure that actual costs correspond to planned costs. Information and action are central to effective cost control.

Cost control is quite a different actitivity to cost reduction and the two must not be confused.

Ensure that specific promotional plan is produced and adhered to:

decide role
set up co-ordination team

Pre-exhibition press contact:

master press list
press releases (translations)
feature articles
press conferences

Pre-exhibition advertising:

single insertions do not represent value for money
consider loose inserts
general invitation cards

Obtain lists of people to meet from:

commercial post
local associations
Chambers of Commerce
directories
overseas agents
direct mail lists

Produce 1st, 2nd, 3rd category lists:

most important potentials
people who influence or make purchases
balance of master list

Keep exhibition stand in public view through:

editorial mentions
press review
regular press coverage during exhibition
special events on stand (films, seminars and receptions)

Use personal contacts and direct mail to get listed people to the stand

Organise effective stand supervision for visitors

Have adequate supplies of information on hand for visitors

Apart from direct selling medium of exhibition use it as general promotional medium

After close of exhibition ensure adequate exploitation of follow up

Co-ordination team:
> report to high enough level
> allocate own budget
> split down cost centres
> utilise outside help (e.g. design and layout)
> check competitors' activities
> decide on press contact
> allocate advertising space
> list people who will probably attend
> set sales, service and information targets
> train staff who will be on stand helping visitors
> organise publicity for use on stand
> set up separate public relations team to maximise results from the exhibition/trade fair

Is it the right exhibition theme?

Should we promote country, product or company?

Should we run our own exhibition/show as an adjunct?

Is there a registration system for subsequent follow up?

Can we invite influential people to our stand?

If we have exhibited there before, what proportion of target audience reached and what was cost per visitor?

The following printed material should be produced:

> show leaflet identifying:
> > exhibitors
> > exhibits
> > companies participating
> > major products
> > plan of exhibits
> VIP invitations
> general invitations or tickets
> special press release header

Stand design — use creative design consultants to design stand and recognised stand builders to erect stand:
> portability afterwards
> total size required
> image to be presented
> durability
> use of area within stand

3.25 ANALYSIS OF EXHIBITION AND TRADE FAIR RESULTS

First analyse all requests or messages into the main action groups:

    sales
    service
    information
    other

Then check following:

    visitor buying power
    composition and competence of stand team
    competitor's exhibits
    quality for overall exhibition
    opportunities for publicity
    public relations opportunities

Consider mailings of selected people who:
    visited exhibition
    asked for tickets
    visited your stand

Check overall expenditure:
    travel
    hotel
    entertainment
    space cost
    stand building cost
    publicity

Compare sales with previous exhibitions/trade fair

Check sales achieved against targeted sales

Organise moratorium to be attended by stand personnel/co-ordination team/senior management/other interested people

Check original cost budgets against actual and analyse and explain variances

4   Manufacture

The following questions need to be asked:

Do adequate standards exist?

Are performance records adequate?

Are variances promptly reported and fully investigated?

If some employees perform both direct and indirect activities, is the system for distinguishing the time spent on each adequate?

Are all processing operations necessary?

Could alternative processes be used to advantage?

Could existing processes be simplified?

Is the sequence of operations the best possible?

Is idle time between operations at a minimum?

Can operations be performed in different departments to avoid handling delays?

Do any operations result in excessive rejects?

Are required completion dates shown on production orders?

In scheduling production is sufficient lead time allowed to enable the accumulation of small orders?

Do we minimise set up costs by allowing sufficient lead time?

Could we schedule labour more efficiently with long production lead times?

Are we sure that special processing requirements can be fitted in, with a sufficiently small lead time?

Are alternative processing methods developed and used for scheduling standard operations in bottleneck areas?

Are cost differences between alternate processing methods known?

Are machine loadings used for production scheduling?

Are workloads planned sufficiently far in advance to permit work force and machines to be balanced?

How much idle time and overtime occurred in the previous period/year?

How much was anticipated?

How much subcontracting was done last year?

Why was this required?

Is scrap/spoilage a significant element of production cost?

Is there a sound procedure for disposing of scrap?

Is scrap sold on the basis of bids?

Are records of spoilage maintained for control purposes?

Are all categories of cost in the manufacturing sphere planned in advance?

Are these the specified responsibility of named individuals?

Does the company employ a flexible budgeting procedure?

Is the inventory of maintenance spares adequate?

Are shortages excessive in the light of the total investment?

General questions that need to be asked:

Are quotations obtained from a number of sources?

Are alternative suppliers approached?

Are all purchase requisitions/purchase orders properly authorised?

Does a policy exist for inviting bids/estimates /tenders?

Are safeguards in existence to prevent the purchasing of excessive quantities?

Is the purchasing department given a sound forecast of materials and other requirements in good time to enable them to be bought on favourable terms?

Are some components currently being made that could be bought from outside at less cost?

Ordering costs against stock-holding costs?

Do buyers have the authority to speculate in commodity markets?

Financial questions that need to be asked:

What are the vendor's financial and credit ratings?

What credit terms are offered?

How do these compare with other suppliers' credit terms?

How do they compare with the suppliers' cash flow needs?

What are the cost implications of overdue deliveries?

Are make or buy studies undertaken?

Are the prices competitive (given quality levels)?

What controls do suppliers have over their activities?

Is standard costing employed?

Is sufficient information available by specific cost element to know the reasonableness of the price quoted?

Might past termination or redetermination data be helpful in analysing this procurement?

Is the price reasonable in terms of competition?

What is the suppliers current financial position as shown in the most recent balance sheet?

What is the suppliers current and projected levels of business?

Are there additional sources of capital if they are needed (for the supplier)?

What type of accounting system is employed — job cost? standard cost? other?

Price breakdowns by cost element on fixed price contracts should be furnished

Is there any objection to contracting on other than a fixed price basis?

Is cost accumulated by lot release, and how are initial production costs estimated?

Is special tooling being purchased separately?

Are there any mating interchangeability problems?

Should tooling be coded?

Have we distinguished between special tooling required for the contract and facility items?

How are labour costs accounted for?

Are operations covered by time standards? If so, how are they established?

Does he employ learning curves in projecting labour costs? If so, what rate of learning does he employ?

Are learning curves employed in projecting labour costs? If so, what rate of learning are employed?

Are supplier's employees unionised? If so, when do union contracts expire?

Will designated individuals in engineering, production, and finance be specified from whom the buyer can obtain pertinent information and data as he requires it?

Are all necessary activities included?

Check realistic control points and flow-times have been established

Has he balanced loads among activities so that production will proceed without delay?

Are there any special handling, packaging or shipping requirements that may delay delivery?

Are spares involved, and are they allowed for in the vendor's plans and schedules?

Are all inspection, test, and engineering requirements fully understood?

Is the item adequately described on the blue-prints specification, purchase order etc?

Are there any special test or quality control requirements the vendor must meet?

Does he fully understand them, and does he have the time, facilities and know-how to comply?

Are sources accustomed to manufacturing this item?

Do they demonstrate ability to meet this schedule?

Do their past rejection experiences demonstrate ability to meet test and quality requirements?

Is a performance bond advisable?

Should the right be obtained to use or acquire tooling, designs, materials to manufacture the item in case of default?

Are supply costs of consumable production materials properly isolated from general maintenance costs?

Are supplies purchased in economic quantities?

Are there safeguards against overstocking?

Do excessive material shortages arise?

Are obsolete supplies disposed of?

Is there adequate protection against pilferage and wastage?

Are containers compatible with storage, and materials handling?

Is the most suitable materials handling equipment used?

Can materials be moved best by gravity or on rollers?

Is a conveyor justified?

Are fork-lift trucks and pallets used to advantage?

Are the materials handling and manufacturing functions effectively co-ordinated?

Where should in-coming and out-going materials be located with respect to work stations?

Can operations be combined at one work station to reduce materials handling?

Are containers uniform to permit stacking?

Can pallatised loads be used?

Could lighter or low cost packaging be used?

Is shrink wrapping possible with current advance in technology?

Is packaging design co-ordinated with materials handling?

Do all items really need packages?

Are scrap and waste materials dealt with effectively?

Are containers marked/coloured for easier segregation/identification?

Could materials be purchased in sizes or quantities that would make for easier materials handling?

How much capital is tied up in obsolete materials/components?

Could excess stocks be sold in bulk with special discounts, or is it cheaper to allow high stocks to run down through normal usage?

How much of inventory investment is in work-in-progress?

What are the costs of carrying each type of inventory?

What are the costs of reordering items for inventory?

Are order points developed for each item on the basis of lead times, rates of usage, and safety stocks?

If of value, are returnable containers properly accounted for and controlled?

Could a deposit system be used for returnable containers/pallets?

Are incoming goods examined for quantity, quality and conformance to order?

Has an analysis been carried out to verify lead times used in reordering?

Where sales are seasonal is it more advisable to produce in accordance with demand, or to produce at an even rate, and use stocks as a buffer?

Who are the key people in the vendor's organisation?

What are their titles and functions?

What is the average experience and educational level in each department or group?

What are the vendor's design and development procedures?

How does he incorporate design changes?

How does he integrate tooling and manufacturing techniques with research and development activities?

Will he comply with the buyer's engineering standards and procedures for items made to buyer design, and will he produce drawings on buyer format when he requests it?

What are the vendor's inspection procedures and controls?

How frequently does he calibrate tools, gauges, and test equipment for meeting primary engineering standards?

How does he control test equipment furnished to subcontractors?

Does he have a separate Reliability Engineering or Quality Control function?

Where does it report, and how is it organised?

What is the scope of its activity?

What is the nature of the planning, scheduling, and inventory control systems?

How are requirements released — by job, by lot, by forecast?

How is production performance reported (actual versus scheduled)?

Who is production performance reported by and is the level high enough to ensure few problems?

Can the frequency of performance reporting be increased to limit possible future problems?

How does the vendor control and incorporate engineering changes?

Who is responsible for machine and manpower loading?

Does the vendor forecast loads, and is there a procedure for comparing current loads against forecast?

What is his system of stock and material control?

How does he identify and separate materials?

How does he dispose of scrap, surplus and obsolete materials?

What are his procedures of in-process inspection and quality control?

What is the procedure of receiving inspection?

Does he require certifications or test approvals from his suppliers? If so, for what items of purchase?

Are spares involved? If so, are they allowed for in plans and schedules?

What are the quality control arrangements?

Financial checks on supplier's capability:
  use credit reference agency
  inspect previous balance sheets
  bank/accountants references
  trade references
  individual references on Directors
  check credit terms offered
  ask other buyers

Decentralised v Centralised Purchasing

Decentralised purchasing:
  faster reaction time
  awareness of local conditions
  closer to plant management
  better if many product lines
  tight delivery times
  large company with separate divisions

Centralised purchasing:
  strong control
  economies of bulk purchase

Note: Decentralised purchasing can only succeed with a good structural management system
Centralised purchasing if imposed on a completely decentralised company will not work because divisions will want to keep their own autonomy

Discounts:
  always ask for discount
  take discount if offered even if terms of payment are not strictly adhered to
  check to see if other suppliers (or even divisions within own supplier's company) offer discounts
  offer prompt payment if discount offered (after goods delivered)

4.6 VALUE IMPROVEMENT

Manufacturer v Customer

- improved product design without changing quality or use
- material substitutions
- better production methods
- lowered material costs by better price negotiations
- remove unnecessary characteristics, both functional and quality

- reduced product price but no quality and functional use
- improved product quality
- additional characteristics to improve functional use

Value improvement can be achieved under the following main headings:

Price analysis:
  best possible price while still allowing a reasonable profit
  identify elements of highest costs to incite improvement action on the vendor's part
  identify any possible hidden charges or unnecessary cost factors
  detect any poor specifications that increase costs and price

Procurement research:
  Analysis of trends of cost and usage
  better buying plans
  specification changes
  reduced shortages because of co-ordinated buying

Design analysis:
  using purchasing knowledge
  using vendor feedback

4.7 PURCHASING EFFECTIVENESS REPORTS

Progress reports can cover:

  Reduced vendor prices through negotiations
  Improved practice — blanket ordering, systems purchasing, order consolidation
  Savings — e.g. tooling costs, freight charges, cash discounts
  Substitutions of less costly material
  Quantity discounts
  Phased-out deliveries, and/or economical ordering quantities
  Standardised material or better parts specifications enabling less costly material use or more choice of vendors
  Using close suppliers, to reduce warehouse space used
  Better packaging, palletised purchases, reusable/lighter containers
  New buying sources
  Recommendations on changing from buying to making, or making to buying
  Taking advantage of price fluctuations
  Simplifying systems and procedures:
      eliminated excess forms
      eliminated unneeded records
      simplified order writing
      grouped orders
      gave better service or information
  Better warranties
  Increases revenue in sales of obsolete, surplus or damaged material

Purchasing effectiveness:

  Ratio of Purchasing to total company personnel
  Purchasing department cost per £ of purchase
  Actual v budgeted cost
  £ savings per £ of purchase
  Variance of actual material cost to standard
  Cost of material
  Cost per Purchase Order
  Number of transactions handled
  % of deliveries late
  % of returned shipments to total
  £'s of discounts earned

4.8 DESIGN REQUIREMENTS

Preliminaries:

> feasibility
> suitability
> composition of product
> aesthetics

Materials:

> economy
> purity
> availability
> quality

> *Note:* could we use new types of materials?

Physical aspects:

> fatigue
> vibration
> shock
> wear
> corrosion
> damp
> dirt

General factors to consider:

> could standard parts be used for the design?
> have we considered the product's future environment?
> what reliability will the customer accept?
> has the ease of manufacture been considered?
> what type of quality control will be required?
> will assembly be easy and cheap?
> what difficulties will there be for routine maintenance and repair?
> is our product up to the general standards of design from competitors?
> will we maximise the design potential (eg Design Council awards) for public relations purposes

4.9 MAKE OR BUY ANALYSIS

Quantifiable factors:

> raw material costs
> scrap percentages as they affect material and labour costs
> learning costs at the start of production
> freight in and incoming inspection on both raw material and purchased parts
> labour needed
> fringe benefit costs on labour
> additional overhead:
>> depreciation
>> maintenance costs
>> spare parts
> tooling costs
> power fuel costs
> additional supervision
> inventory carrying costs
> additional space
> money tied up in space saving equipment
> material handling costs
> plant capacity
> spare factory space availability

Non-quantifiable factors:

> additional/lessened burden on supervision and higher management
> quality and delivery performance of vendors
> need for an assured source
> need to safeguard designs or process secrets
> aim of employment stability
> possession of needed skills
> raw material availability
> foreseeable and suspected technological change
> effect on existing suppliers and their relationship to the purchaser
> government reaction
> trade union involvement
> involvement of outside countries and foreign government
> press reaction

4.10 INVENTORY MANAGEMENT

The major factors in inventory acquisition are:

Purchased parts:
     purchasing department costs
     freight inwards
     receiving department costs
     incoming inspection
     portion of warehouse labour involved in
     putting away
     personnel involved in accounts payable

Manufactured parts:
     set-up labour
     start-up material and/or scrap
     first piece and later inspection
     cost of preparing a manufacturing order

Inventory carrying costs elements are:

     insurance
     taxes
     space
     material handling
     return on investment
     physical inventorying
     loss, damage and deterioration
     obsolescence
     economic trends
     optional miscellaneous items:
          record keeping and accounting
          management charges

Economic Order Quantity:

Balance cost of placing order to cost of inventory
holding =

$$\frac{\text{Annual usage (£'s) x Cost placing order}}{\text{Cost of holding material}}$$

4.11 EDP IN PURCHASING

Possible savings:

     removes routine work
     enables orders to be consolidated
     data enables better negotiation
     measure of work load
     purchase progress report initiated or im-
     proved
     small orders can be highlighted

To determine the design requirements of any
electronic data processing system, consider the
following:

     number of different items ordered per year
     number of different transactions per year
     amount of money spent per item per year
     price quotations by item and supplier
     price history record by item
     list of current suppliers for any given item or
     group of items
     categorise items by value, i.e. A-B-C analysis
     calculate economic order quantity and
     compare with price break points
     generate the purchase order upon stock
     depletion below an indicated point
     check vendor's order acknowledgment
     list open orders — by buyer, by due date, and
     in total
     note receipt of material against the order
     compare invoices with receiving report and
     with the order, and print the check, if they
     agree
     vendor performance on delivery and quality

Consider the use of:
     in-house data processing staff to write
     programme
     outside time sharing bureau
     ready made 'off the shelf' package

Failure costs:

- scrap
- rework
- reinspection
- sorting of rejects
- losses on sale of substandard items
- servicing of customers' complaints
- extra operations
- selective assembly
- downtime
- after sales service (under guarantee or warranty)
- lost sales opportunities

Appraisal costs:

- incoming materials
- manufacturing processes
- products at all stages of manufacture and use
- storage facilities
- gauges and measuring devices

Prevention costs:

- special investigations into failure costs
- training personnel in control of quality
- provision of quality reports

Note: The loss of turnover in terms of lost customer goodwill can far outweigh the extra quality control costs or customer basic service expenditure

Are quality control standards for all materials, components and products regularly reviewed?

Are tolerances, allowances, finish, and other requirements necessary and appropriate?

Can the specification requirements be raised to improve quality without increasing cost?

Will lowering the specification requirements reduce costs significantly without the loss of quality?

Can quality be improved by using new processes?

Will a change in inspection requirements affect the rate (hence cost) of rejects?

Is defective work excessive?

Are causes of defective work noted?

Is product performance in the field evaluated?

Could quality control costs be reduced (without sacrificing quality) by reducing or eliminating some inspection procedures?

Is the company paying for costly inspection at other sources when these could be more economically performed at the company's own premises?

Are inspection activities scheduled in such a way that they do not hold production up?

Are quality control ideas applied throughout the company rather than being confined to the production sphere?

Do the benefits from using quality control procedures exceed their cost?

Could work study be used to identify area with least (and most) problems regarding quality control?

If areas of least and most can be identified how can some cross-fertilisation of ideas and practices be best effected?

4.14 SAMPLING METHODS

How large a sample should be inspected?

How should the items in the sample chosen for inspection be selected from the total?

When the number of defective items in the sample has been determined how can the number of defective items in the total be estimated?

What is the possible or probable percentage of error in the estimate of the total number of defective items?

What percentage of defective items in the sample is sufficient to justify the rejection of the entire lot?

How can the number of defective items in various samples be charted over time in order that unfavourable trends may be detected and the causes corrected?

Consider the use of time saving terminals linked to large frame computers for the following:
    instant results
    choice of methods
    most accurate answer
    ongoing availability to update with new data
    new and different programmes always available

4.15 LOCATION OF NEW PLANT

Main considerations:

    proximity to raw materials
    fuel and power availability and cost
    transportation
    labour supply
    water supply
    water and disposal facilities
    accommodation
    pollution

Less important:

    market location
    living and social conditions
    proximity to suppliers
    plant maintenance services

Site conditions:

    topography (flat, cheap or zoned, land, sea, lake or river location)
    soil condition
    water supply
    waste disposal
    position of plant to local transport facilities
    availability of homes for workers
    local by-laws, including sanitation, air and stream pollution
    living conditions for labour and management: climate, scenery, recreational facilities, schools, churches, public transport
    community directives for zoning house use and community attitudes towards manufacturing activity

Location — further factors:

    political climate, risk of nationalisation
    integrity of Government controls etc.
    taxation implications
    government grants and common market aid

Factors governing the locating of industry and the relation of new development sites are divided between physical and social elements

4.16 RISK ANALYSIS

The meaning of risk:

> uncertainty creates risk
> risk is the consequence of bad chance
> reducing the uncertainty through better information does not of itself reduce the risk
> the risk in any project may not be a true measure of the risk to an organisation of undertaking the project
> risk is what you stand to lose less what you can afford to lose

Sources of risk:

> risk from insufficient numbers
> risk from misinterpretation
> risk from bias
> risk from external change
> risk from errors of analysis

Analysis of risk:

> risks may be classified according to the way in which they affect forecasting earning power by understating the outlay
> complete failure to break through to the objective
> schedule slippage
> shortening the economic life
> reducing the rate of increase of income
> failing to synchronise with availability of funds

Risk can either be:
> controlled
> not controlled but influenced
> neither controlled nor influenced, but quantified

Funds requirement for any new project:

> new product development
> prototype manufacture and testing
> financing production plant
> providing factory space
> financing stocks of raw materials and components
> initial sales promotion
> stocks in the distribution chain
> losses during the market development phase
> increase in debtor investment after product launch

4.17 INDUSTRIAL SECURITY — FIRE/ BOMB PROTECTION

Protection of critical areas:

> enclosed by physical barriers
> limited access
> guard force on duty
> locks
> intrusion detection devices
> key control system
> package and material control system

Fire protection:

> regulations posted and enforced?
> alarm system in all areas?
> how fast is local Fire Dept.?
> secondary water supply available?
> how much equipment available?
> do you have fire and rescue squads?
> proper storage of combustible material?
> proper training in use of equipment?
> do you have fire drills?
> do you read the Fire Insurance Inspection reports?

Bomb Threats:

> proper channels of communication including reporting procedures
> liaison with law enforcement
> liaison with medical and first aid facilities
> fire procedure
> evacuation procedure
> search procedure
> area to be protected
> determination of company liability in the event of no evacuation
> what factors will weigh in the decision to evacuate or not evacuate?
> post reporting procedures
> procedure to go into effect if there actually is a bomb explosion

Limiting effects of blast:
> wire netting
> bomb curtains (nets) for glass windows
> sand bags/blankets for letter bombs
> X-ray machines for suspicious parcels

General points:

    try to control talking
    destroy carbons
    use special paper
    develop internal alarms
    special conference room
    watch special visitors
    daytime clearing of classified areas
    electronic devices
    false information

Profile of a 'Secret Stealer':

    sudden acquisition of wealth
    possible scandal or rumour surrounding him
    chronic complainer
    heavy drinker or alcoholic
    compulsive gambler
    mentally disturbed
    criminal background
    extensive debts
    narcotics user

Can a recognised security organisation be used to check for bugs in high risk area?

Is disposal of security waste (eg computer print outs) monitored?

Are paper shredders used where possible?

Should security guards be employed to check entrances into building/factory?

Should employee and vehicle search be compulsory on entering work premises?

Is delivery documentation for receipt and despatch of goods adequate?

Are stop and search procedures part of conditions of employment?

Is a regular internal audit made of stores and finished products?

See Also:

5 Distribution and Storage

5.1 WAREHOUSE CONTROL PROCEDURES

Incoming:

> check against documents received
> issue goods received note
> quality control — endorse goods received note

Outgoing:

> check against documents

Order processing

Edit order:
> identify customer
> establish products required
> check delivery date

Record order:
> establish account number
> establish delivery area
> acknowledge order

Credit Control:
> **check credit limit**
> **establish credit outstanding**

Allocate stock:
> notify customer if delay

Retain order until:
> goods available
> delivery due
> van run due

Vehicle route:
> **advice transport section**
> **arrange most cost effective delivery routing**

Picking lists:
> reverse sequence of delivery of goods

Customer delivery notes:
> **date of delivery**
> **signature**

5.2 WAREHOUSE OPERATING EFFICIENCY

Space utilisation efficiency is:

ratio of cubic area occupied to net space available (net — gross space less clearances, stairwells, service facilities)

> could more space be obtained?
> is layout poor with too many aisles?
> would racks help?
> **could goods be stored at work stations?**
> if so, is all the height available being used?
> **can bulk storage be improved?**
> is there a storage plan for each area?
> is warehouse tidy and well stacked?
> re-examine aisles:
>> any unnecessary aisles?
>> if so, how many and where?
>> can they be eliminated or shortened?
>> are aisles in the right places?
>> and laid out for maximum use?
>> **where and how can aisle width be reduced?**
>> **can trucks, stacker cranes be used?**

Handling characteristics:

> ease of handling and stacking
> long materials
> sheet materials
> susceptibility to damage, contamination, infestation
> **special requirements of temperature:**
> humidity

The storage modules adopted are also important. Possible methods include:

> single parts, cartoned or loose
> outer cases, bag and sacks
> **boxes**
> unit loads, pallets and sub-containers
> freight containers
> loose solids and liquids in less than unit loads

5.3 DISTRIBUTION, PACKAGING AND ROUTING

Packaging:

the duration and type of journey involved, and the strains involved

the fragility or perishability of the goods transported

the handling and stacking methods which will be employed at each change in mode

the sensitivity of the goods to environment

the unit value of the goods and how much packaging can be afforded

the extent to which the goods have to be packaged for other reasons

the likelihood of the goods contaminating other goods

the need for identification

the desirability of not having to break down the package for final consignment

the desirability of separate items arriving together at the destination

border documentation and customs requirements

the need to stop pilfering

limitations imposed by doors, hatches, cranes

statutory requirements — e.g. rail packaging regulations, IATA rules

insurance requirements

Routing and scheduling:

number and type of call

capacity of vehicle and vehicle type

urbanisation and vehicle speeds obtainable

balance between driving time and delivery time

size of orders

distance between calls

depot location

maximum working day

shop or customer opening hours

road network

opportunities for return loads

load layout and use of compartments for different products

maintenance of an adequate service level

Logistic Factors:

volume of goods, inwards and outwards

regular deliveries or movements and frequencies

variable deliveries — variants and seasonal effects

trends — increasing or diminishing

customers' expectation of service

type of movement — factory to warehouse, first or second degree outlet or export

Equipment Groups:

manual equipment
sack trucks
stillage trucks
pallet trucks
fixed route equipment
chutes
conveyors
sorting systems
unitised systems
pallet trucks
fork lift trucks
stacker crane

Stock location:

fixed location — bin storage, but this can waste space

random location — least unoccupied space, but increases search time

zoned location — fixed or random located within zones

Manning of warehouse:

evaluate operating requirements of warehouse

study systems and improve where possible

construct job descriptions

perform work study exercise

implement recommendations and improve operating methods

develop incentive schemes where necessary

5.4 PHYSICAL DISTRIBUTION FACILITIES AUDIT

Is the cost per unit changing rapidly on the following:

- transport
- trunking
- local delivery
- warehouse
- local depot
- break-bulk point
- stockholding
- If so, why?

Has the distribution workload (delivery size etc.) changed in level or composition?

Are there changes in technology and environment which upset or challenge the economic basis of the distribution system?

Does the measurement of delivery service show the company to lag behind competition?

Is the company losing sales because of this?

What do our surveys of customer opinion show?

5.5 PHYSICAL DISTRIBUTION FACILITIES

Are depots needed?
If so, how many and where?
How large and with what facilities?
Are central warehouses needed?
If so, how many and where?
How large and with what facilities?
Expanded as trade grows?
Lease v purchase?
How many types of vehicle should be used?
What ancillary equipment should they have?
How many vehicles of each type are required?
How many spare trailers are required for each type of vehicle?
What garaging and workshop facilities are required?
Where should they be located?
What products should be distributed through the system?
Should raw materials, semi-finished goods, supplies, bought-in items, be distributed through the warehouses?
What customers should receive their orders through the system?
What unit-load handling policy should be adopted?
Should the system make use of trunking?
Which products should be stocked in which warehouses and/or depots?
Which customers should receive their orders from which depots?
Should they be served from more than one depot?
Which customers should receive their orders direct from a warehouse or factory?
Under what circumstances could other customers receive their orders direct?
Which warehouses should be supplied from which factories?
Which depots should be supplied from which warehouses and/or factories?
Under what circumstances, if at all, should the warehouses be used as 'shunt' or transit warehouses?
What frequency of service should customers receive?
What minimum order-to-delivery interval should the customers be allowed?

Types of distribution methods:

Rail:
    own trucks
    British Rail trucks
Road:
    company fleet
    leased fleet
    contract fleet
    individual carriers

Canal:
    barges

Ships:
    purchase
    contract

Air:
    contract

What combinations of the above give best distribution methods?
How many types of different means should be used to maximise cost effectiveness?

The average volume of goods demanded by product and geographical location
The marginal profit associated with the sale of the various products after allowing for all other marginal costs *except* distribution
The expected growth in product demand
The seasonal or other cyclical character of the product demands
The random day-to-day fluctuations in the product demands
The physical characteristics of products
The number and location of factories
The number and geographical location of customers to be delivered to
The ordering behaviour of customers including the frequency and size of orders
The cost characteristics of road transport, including capital costs, mileage dependent running costs, standing charges and other time dependent costs, and their dependence on whether the vehicles are owned, leased, contracted or short-term hired
The physical characteristics of possible vehicles, including, in particular, their weight and volume capacities
Distances and times to travel between locations in the system
Loading and/or unloading times at factories, warehouses, depots and customers
The costs of other means of transport
The dependence of transport costs on warehouse and depot facilities and vice versa
One-off costs associated with changing the distribution system
Restrictions on manpower, land and other resources available at the possible warehouse and depot sites and the capacities
Restrictions on capital funds available

The characteristics of the existing system
The uncertainty associated with estimating the value of these factors under future circumstances

Other constraints:
  company policy
  local authorities
  government
  law restrictions
  trade unions
  customers
  competitors
  formal agreements
  informal understandings

Compare costs of company-owned transport function with outside contractors?

Are the best means of transport (cost and service viewpoints) used for different products?

Are increases in transport costs considered to be unavoidable and thus passed on to customers without studying the efficiency of transport activities?

Are *all* transport costs accounted for under the heading of transport?

Can those vehicles having disproportionately high operating costs (in relation to other vehicles of the same make, age, and capacity) be identified?

How are standards set in the transport sphere? (If there are no standards, should they be introduced?)

Is control over fuel exercised by having a bulk storage facility, or does the company rely on outside agencies?

Could the costs be reduced by hiring a fleet (contract or lease) rather than owning vehicles?

Is maintenance planned or available on a crisis basis?

Does the cost control system reveal the extent to which transport facilities are under-utilised?

Does an established procedure exist for scheduling and routing vehicles?

Does routing take into account different road types, urban areas?

Is the most expensive resource (e.g. driver or vehicle) the focus of attention?

Is the capacity constraint of the fleet, volume or weight? (Are right sizes of vehicles in use?)

Can mechanical loading/unloading methods be employed with the type of vehicles in use?

How is performance measured? Which aspects of performance are measured? Driver performance, driver utilisation, vehicle utilisation, delay time?

What follow-up results from the extraction of variances?

Who takes responsibility for the cost of special deliveries?

To what extent can use be made of existing forms/reports (such as log sheets, mileage records etc.) in building up costs?

What exceptions should be made to the usual arrangements?

What inter-company movements frequency standards should be adopted?

What vehicle types should work what routes?

What characteristics should the journey patterns and consequent vehicle schedules have?

What should be the maximum time away from base allowed?

What maintenance and replacement policy should be adopted in respect of the vehicles?

During what hours should the depots, warehouses and factory despatch points operate?

On what routes, with which vehicles, and under what circumstances should multiple shift working of the transport fleet take place?

How much staff and labour is required to operate the transport fleet, the warehouses, the depots, the factory despatch points?

What management structure should be adopted?

Where should 'picking and packing' of customers' orders take place?

Should different arrangements be made for export orders?

What arrangements should be made for setting stock action levels, and monitoring and allocating stocks?

What arrangements should be made for the physical process of raising customers' orders, acknowledgments, despatch notes etc.?

What other control documentation and procedures are required?

What is the broad specification of the management information system required?

What percentage of total sales for each product is directly transacted with users?

What is the history of the introduction of the product and the sequence of marketing steps which led to its present distribution?

What is the replenishment lead time?

What is the history of "out-of-stock" situations?

What stocks are normally held at the plant? Average or seasonal?

What stocks are normally in the distributive pipeline?

is a new warehouse needed?
how much flexibility is needed in the face of
changed markets and equipment?
how much room for expansion?
old or new premises?
what are the design objectives?

Warehouse design objectives long v short term:

minimise need to extend the building
in the next x years
v
minimise capital expenditure by building
only for present needs

enable changes in the layout to be made easily
and cheaply by having large roof spans
v
minimise capital expenditure by using cheapest
spacing of stanchions

minimise building maintenance costs by using
better, more expensive materials in the
construction
v
minimise capital expenditure by using lower
quality (cheaper) materials

minimise labour costs
v
minimise equipment costs

Site selection:

planning regulations, the availability of
services, electricity, gas, water, waste
disposal, plus repair services for specialised
equipment
the availability of transport, in addition to
road and motorway access, good rail, sea,
or canal services may be needed
the availability of labour
any government controls or special grants
which are applicable
the level of local taxes

Parameters for new building design:

what vehicles are used at present
handling equipment required
manoeuvrability of trucks
deck lights
number loading points
number handling bays
possible use of containerisation

Future changes in vehicles:

size of marshalling area
doorway size (draughtproofing and structural problems if too large)
height — note clearances and stocking
height required
illumination levels
sprinklers
services required (steam, air, electricity,
water, fans etc.)
floor loading — reinforcement, if any
columns — integrate within storage areas, if
possible

5.9 NEGOTIATIONS

Know what you want — both the major and minor objectives of your transaction

Don't play the negotiation 'by ear'

Know what the seller would be satisfied in achieving

Open up the negotiations by a discussion of mutual interest

Avoid making first demands, proposals, or even positive assertions or claims

Negotiation is in a very real sense a test of strength so the buyer should strive to avoid a pattern of concession

Introduce trading points at the outset, i.e. those points that you can concede later

Never give anything away, seek counter-concessions in exchange

Know what limitations are imposed on the seller-negotiator

Don't make the buyer lose face on a point and therefore lose an ally

Seek technical assistance and support where necessary

Admit your own shortcomings and seek help

If negotiations are conducted by a team make sure that all the members are on the same team

In a team let the team leader lead

Always have a dry run with team negotiations

Be sensitive to the emotional temperature of the negotiation — lower the temperature when necessary

Minimise emotional involvement by always sticking to the facts

Avoid hearsay, personal opinion

Be conscious of the psychology of the negotiation:

> Give the buyer prestige and importance
> Never argue — be cool, calm and calculating
> Keep your eyes and ears open

5.10 VEHICLE SECURITY PROCEDURES

Background check on drivers
Saturation of area with guard personnel
Internal alarms in truck
Meter in truck giving mileage, time, speed
Modern freight forms — bills of lading etc.
Locking and disabling devices
Use of seals
Large numbers on roof of truck
Secure loading areas
Dock surveillance by closed circuit TV
Road patrols
Check-in points along route
Telephone in cab
Planted merchandise
Secretly labelled objects detected by X-ray
Firearms should not be carried by driver

See Also:

6 Personnel

6.1 PERSONNEL ACTIVITIES

Manpower planning

Recruitment

Selection

Training:
    induction
    on the job
    managerial

Promotions

Transfers

Redundancies

Short time working

Discipline interviews

Grievance settlements

Personnel records

Wage/Salary policies

Job analysis/evaluation

Incentive & Profit-sharing scheme

Loan schemes

Fringe benefits:
    life insurance
    health insurance
    accident insurance
    pensions
    share incentives

Safety programmes

Recreational facilities

Canteen facilities

Company housing

Plant security

Company publications

Notice boards

Industrial relations

Charitable donations

Executive development

6.2 ROLE OF THE PERSONNEL FUNCTION

Is the role of the personnel function defined?

Has the organisation developed personnel policies to serve as continuing guide-lines on personnel matters in the following areas:

    quality of managers, staff and hourly paid employees
    levels of remuneration (pay and fringe benefits compared with market rates) and constant review
    amount and scope of training schemes
    promotion and the extent to which the organisation intends to rely on promotion from within
    employee relations:
        recognition of unions
        the rights of union or employee representatives
        the extent to which employees should be kept informed on and consulted about plans and policies
        the approach used for dealing with disciplinary and grievance problems, including the extent to which appeals can be made and the use of external conciliation or arbitration procedures
        redundancy — the basis for deciding who should be made redundant, the amount of notice, levels of payment and the degree to which prior consultation should take place
        safety, health and welfare the degree to which the organisation wishes to go beyond statutory obligations concerning the health and safety and provide welfare and recreational facilities

Is the personnel function carrying out any activities which more properly should be carried out elsewhere in the organisation?

Is the organisation structure of the personnel function suitable for fulfilling its roles and carrying out its activities?
    is the head of the function in a position to exert sufficient influence over the formulation and implementation of personnel policies?

are individuals in positions within the function given explicit information on the main activities that they should carry out?

are individuals given sufficient authority to carry out their duties?

have standards of performance and targets been established wherever possible for members of the function?

is there any overlap between the responsibilities of individuals?

Recommended structure:

Personnel director — responsible to the main board for all aspects of personnel with some or all of the following key people responsible to him:

> Personnel manager
> Training manager
> Security advisor
> House journal editor
> Canteen manager
> Industrial relations advisor

Establish the future need for personnel by number and quality of employees on the basis of the manpower plan

Establish job descriptions for all managerial positions

Conduct appointment interviews, evaluate candidates. Recommend new appointments to line management

Develop and administer a wage and salary structure, including salary brackets for each position and with fringe and other benefit packages

Introduce and service a system of appraisal of all employees by the superior, as a basis for promotion and planning the filling of vacancies

In conjunction with line management, identify employees suitable as successors to the present management

Develop and administer internal and external training programmes, so that employees can become familiar with modern methods

Work out individual training programmes (attendance at courses and seminars, job rotation) for managers and future managers worthy of promotion

Administer all personnel records

Organise and administer the social programmes
> pension fund
> life insurance
> medical aid
> canteen
> sports club
> welfare
> insurances

Organise and administer suggestion schemes

Represent the firm in matters relating to:
> works council
> trade unions
> employment law
> accident prevention
> with assistance from other specialist functions

Observe morale in the firm and take steps to keep it as high as possible

Contact with employers' federations and employment officers at universities and colleges

Limitation of responsibilities:

The personnel manager is responsible for ensuring that the firm has at all times the right number and quality of employees

He cannot appoint, dismiss or promote anyone or award any increase in wages or salary without the consent of the line manager concerned

He cannot make any alterations in the organisation structure of the firm without the consent of the manager concerned

The salary policies of a company provide the basis upon which its salary structure and salary administration procedures are developed. The main areas are:

basic philosophy
the importance attached by the organisation to the total remuneration package as the means of attracting, motivating and retaining staff

market rates
the extent to which market rates will be allowed to influence the salary structure and the level of salaries within the organisation in relation to market rates

equity
the degree to which the organisation is going to strive after internal pay relativities between jobs will be established and maintained

reward system
the specific role of financial rewards and incentives as part of the reward system

salary structure
the degree to which this should be formalised and the design of the salary structure; that is, the number and width of the salary brackets and the amount of overlap, if any, between salary brackets

incremental system
the use of salary increments to provide rewards

incentive scheme
the use of bonus and profit sharing schemes to provide incentive

flexibility
the amount of discretion that managers will be allowed to fix salary levels for jobs, determine starting rates or award promotional or merit increments

total remuneration
the best mix of basic salary and other benefits

communication
the amount of information given to staff, collectively or individually, about salary policies

6.5 SALARY ADMINISTRATION

Salary administration procedures are concerned with the implementation and control of salary policies and with the control of salary costs against budgets.

The aims must be:

serve the aims and objectives of the undertaking as a whole

ensure that a sufficient number of suitable people are attracted to join the undertaking

encourage suitable staff to remain in its employment

provide appropriate rewards for good performance and incentives for further improvements in performance

achieve equity in the pay for similar jobs and consistency in the differentials that exist between different levels of jobs in accordance with their relative value

provide not only for fairness in the operation of the salary system but also for staff to be convinced that the system is fair

operate flexibly enough to accommodate changes in the relative market rates for different skills and in the organisation of the undertaking

achieve simplicity in operation as an aid to staff understanding and to minimise administrative effort

ensure that the salary policies are consistent with the requirements of Government and with the public interest

achieve these aims at the least cost to the undertaking

6.6 BASIC FEATURES OF A SALARY STRUCTURE

All jobs are allocated into a salary grade within the structure on the basis of an assessment of their internal and external value to the organisation.

Each salary grade consists of a salary bracket or band. No individuals holding a job in the grade can go beyond the maximum of the salary band unless he or she is promoted.

Jobs can be regraded within the structure when it is decided that their value has altered because of a change in responsibilities or a pronounced movement in the market rate for the job.

General increases in the cost of living or in market rates are dealt with by proportionate increases to the maxima and minima of salary bands.

The salary bands are wide enough to provide room to progress individual salaries in relation to performance and in accordance with the level of the job. At junior clerical levels the band could be no wider than 15 per cent to 20 per cent. At supervisory and managerial levels the bands could be between 35 per cent and 60 per cent but the most typical width is 50 per cent.

A differential between each salary band which provides adequate scope for rewarding increased responsibility on promotion to the next higher grade but does not create too wide a gap between adjacent grades and thus reduce the amount of flexibility available for grading jobs. This should normally be between 15 per cent and 25 per cent but 20 per cent is probably a typical differential.

An overlap between bands which allows very experienced individuals in a grade to be paid more than inexperienced individuals in the next higher grade.

All jobs allocated into a salary grade are assumed to be broadly of the same level. In other words, they normally have the same minimum and maximum rates which correspond with the grade boundaries. If there are any exceptions to this rule in the shape of jobs with a higher minimum or lower maximum salary, they should be specified.

Progression within a grade depends on the performance of the individual. It would generally be assumed that all fully competent individuals in any jobs in a grade would eventually reach the normal maximum of the grade, if they are not promoted out of it. Less competent individuals may stop progressing at some point below the grade maximum. In some circumstances, provision may be made for exceptional individuals to receive more than the normal maximum.

SALARY BANDS

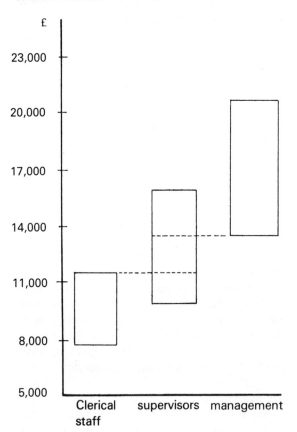

Preference for a fixed rather than a variable system of remuneration related to the following:

the acceptance of a relationship between length of service in a job and value to the organisation, especially in jobs which require a training or probationary period

the fairness of such systems and their freedom from the arbitrary use of management discretion

the mere size and geographical distribution of individual departments, as well as the need, under any system, to keep the standards of granting increments in line, as between one department and another, may present difficulties

the existence of only limited scope for variations in job performance or special difficulties in measuring performance

the motivational value of fixed systems in situations where it is felt to be of primary importance to emphasise teamwork and co-operative attitudes rather than individual competitiveness

the ease with which fixed incremental systems can be administered

the support of fixed systems by the trade unions, who generally believe that pay arrangements should be defined and made explicit to the maximum possible extent and express doubts about the fairness of any incremental scheme which is based on performance assessment

the proven acceptability of the system over a long period

The arguments in favour of variable incremental schemes are as follows:

they provide an effective basis for motivation by relating pay to performance

they allow management discretion in the award of salary increases they are inherently cost-effective, not simply in the sense of restraining costs but of ensuring that increases are related to assessed contributions

they provide more flexibility to match pay to the individual in the face of greater job mobility and changing conditions

managers prefer to feel that increased effectiveness will bring commensurate rewards

Profit sharing schemes endeavour to achieve one or more of the following objectives:

> to encourage employees to identify themselves more closely with the company by developing a common concern for its progress

> to stimulate a greater interest amongst employees in the affairs of the company as a whole

> to encourage better co-operation between management and employees

> to recognise that employees of the company have a moral right to share in the profits they have helped to produce

> to demonstrate in practical terms the goodwill of the company towards its employees

Schemes which share profits according to some universal formula amongst all or most employees may not provide any real incentive because they fail to satisfy the three basic requirements of an incentive scheme, namely:

> that the reward should bear a direct relation to the effort

> that the payment should follow immediately or soon after the effort

> that the method of calculation should be simple and easily understood

Types of Schemes:

> The main types of profit sharing schemes are:

> **immediate cash** — a proportion of profits is paid direct to employees in cash as soon as profits are determined

> **immediate shares** — profits are distributed direct to employees in the form of stock as soon as the profits are determined

> **deferred cash** — profits are credited to employee accounts to be paid at retirement or in other stated circumstances

The amount of reward received after tax should be sufficiently high to encourage staff to accept a high and exacting standard of performance.

Standard bonuses should not be less than ten per cent of the base salary and, if the circumstances demand an effective incentive, the standard bonus should be around 20 per cent of salary.

The incentive arrangement should, as far as possible, be related to criteria over which the individual has a substantial measure of control.

Any criteria used should preferably be measurable in quantifiable terms. The best criteria are financial ones.

The scheme should be sensitive enough to ensure that rewards are proportionate to achievements.

The individual should be able to calculate the reward he would receive for a given level of achievement.

The scheme should be acceptable to and benefit the company as well as the participants.

The scheme should operate in conjunction with a sound salary structure in which individuals are paid according to the level of responsibility carried in their job.

The scheme should be easy to administer and to understand and it should be tailored to meet the requirements of the company operating it.

Constraints should be built into the scheme which ensure that staff cannot receive inflated bonuses which may not be directly related to their own efforts.

The formula for calculating the bonus and the conditions under which it is paid should be clearly defined.

The scheme should contain provisions for a regular review, say every two or three years, which could result in the scheme being changed or discontinued.

Bonus Schemes for Senior Executives:

Incentive bonus schemes vary widely in complexity, size of bonus paid and the number and level of staff covered.

The majority of schemes in operation in the United Kingdom use some measure of company profitability to determine bonus although additional criteria are sometimes incorporated in the scheme.

The main types of schemes are:
bonus fund scheme

individual bonus scheme related to company profitability

individual bonus scheme related to an individual target

The main advantages:

they provide participants with a stake in the company which should increase their commitment to its interests

the reward is related to growth in company profitability and its status in the market

an increase in share price benefits both the participating employees and the shareholders

they are potentially a useful device in high risk situations, especially when directors or executives are involved in new ventures or in turning round loss situations

possible taxation advantages which may exist from time to time

The main disadvantages:

the actual size of the gain may be difficult to forecast

staff are generally unable to relate the size of the reward to their own performance

the size of the reward may be subject to stock market fluctuations which are not connected with the performance of the company

the rewards will not be received for a number of years

it is not possible to predict accurately the tax situation when shares are encashed

the scheme needs to be approved by shareholders in General Meeting;

institutional investors have set ownership guidelines for share schemes

if restricted to executives, they are socially divisive and increase the 'we/they' attitudes — the Government savings-related scheme introduced in 1973 was an attempt to overcome this problem

there is no proof that these schemes do increase identification and commitments

Comparison with the advantages of Bonus Schemes:

bonus schemes may be more easily designed to relate both to company profitability and to individual performance

it is normally easy to calculate the reward received for a given level of performance

approval is not required from the shareholders

the tax situation is relatively straightforward

the company retains greater control of the rewards given to individual staff

a bonus scheme can be discontinued at any time and limits can be imposed which restrict the maximum bonus payable

6.11 NEED FOR MANAGEMENT DEVELOPMENT AND MANPOWER PLANNING

Management Development

Is there any evidence that:

the organisation is finding it difficult to provide for management succession, i.e. to fill from within management vacancies arising from expansion, promotion, retirement, death or wastage?

the performance of individual managers or groups of managers needs to be improved in general or in particular areas?

Are records maintained of:

the future needs of the organisation for managers?

the names of individuals who have potential for promotion?

Have any formal plans been made to provide for management succession and to improve the performance of existing managers by:

counselling individual managers and preparing career development and training plans for them?

training programmes using internal and/or external courses?

job rotation?

Manpower Planning

In general is needed when:

a new section, department or site is to be opened, closed or re-organised

an organisation expands or contracts

sections of staff or other workforce approach retirement

jobs are re-designed through introduction of new technology of production methods or their expected development, reliance is placed on specialist employees in a scarce labour market or recruitment generally

promotion and career planning is necessary for greater job satisfaction and motivation

6.12 ELEMENTS OF A MANPOWER PLAN

MANPOWER REQUIREMENTS
REPLACEMENT RECRUITMENT

▲ SALES — DEMAND REQUIREMENTS
- PRESENT AREA —
  - EXISTING PRODUCTS
    - PRESENT STAFF — LEAVERS → ADDITIONAL STAFF
  - NEW PRODUCTS → ADDITIONAL STAFF
- NEW AREA —
  - EXISTING PRODUCTS
  - NEW PRODUCTS

▲ DISTRIBUTION — AREA COVERED
- PRESENT AREA
  - PRESENT STAFF — LEAVERS → ADDITIONAL STAFF
- NEW AREA → ADDITIONAL STAFF

▲ PRODUCTION — AVAILABLE CAPACITY
- EXISTING PRODUCTS
  - EXISTING TECHNIQUES —
    - PRESENT STAFF — LEAVERS
  - NEW TECHNIQUES — PRESENT STAFF — LEAVERS → ADDITIONAL STAFF
- NEW PRODUCTS
  - EXISTING TECHNIQUES — PRESENT STAFF — LEAVERS
  - NEW TECHNIQUES — PRESENT STAFF — LEAVERS → ADDITIONAL STAFF

▲ ADMINISTRATION — SERVICE LEVEL
- PRESENT SYSTEMS
  - PRESENT STAFF — LEAVERS
  - PRESENT STAFF — LEAVERS
- NEW SYSTEMS → ADDITIONAL STAFF

Are adequate manpower records maintained which show:

> the numbers employed in each main occupational category?
> the age distribution of employees?
> the turnover of employees analysed by occupation and reason for leaving?

Are forecasts made of future manpower requirements in terms of numbers and skills for each of the main occupational groups?

Are the forecasts based on reliable data concerning:
> factors affecting the demand for manpower, for example:
>> expansions or contractions in activities carried out by the organisation as shown in corporate plans
>> future changes in technology or methods of working
> factors affecting the supply of manpower, for example:
>> promotions
>> retirements
>> wastage from within the organisation
>> the availability of suitable manpower from outside

Are functional and/or departmental forecasts of manpower requirements obtained on a regular basis and collated to form an overall manpower plan?

Are manpower forecasts translated into realistic plans for satisfying requirements by:

> recruitment
> re-deployment
> training or re-training
> improving the utilisation or improving the productivity of employees

Are recruitment programmes based on manpower plans?

Is any attempt made to reduce the number of employees to be recruited from external sources by:
> introducing measures to reduce labour turnover?
> improving the utilisation and productivity of employees?
> training or re-training employees?
> promoting or transferring employees?

Are standardised procedures laid down for:
> submitting and approving requisitions for staff?
> advertising?
> obtaining references?

Are standard job descriptions and man specifications available for each of the main categories of employees who are recruited regularly?

Have the personnel staff and the managers responsible for interviewing applicants been trained in interviewing techniques?

Are selection tests used?
If so, have they been properly evaluated to ensure that they are both valid and reliable?

Do interviewers conduct a properly structured interview based on job descriptions and man specifications and using defined criteria for assessing candidates?

Is there any evidence that there are undue delays in completing the recruitment procedures and filling vacancies?
If so, why?

Are there any problems in recruiting the number or quality of employees required?
If so, why?

Are all possible sources of recruits explored thoroughly, for example:
    universities
    technical colleges
    schools
    the armed services
    employment exchanges
    agencies
    friends
    relations of employees
    ex-employees

Are any other methods of attracting applicants used, for example:
    direct mail
    exhibitions
    tours of the company
    visits to universities
    schools

Is enough effort being made to produce a favourable image of the organisation as a place in which to work by maintaining contact with universities, schools and employment agencies, by press publicity and by the use of recruitment literature?

Are induction programmes in use which give new employees adequate information about:
    terms and conditions of employment
    history of company
    structure of organisation
    products produced with brief descriptions
    introduction to senior management

Has the organisation clearly defined training policies covering:
    the objectives of training?
    the scope of the training schemes?
    the limitations of expenditure on training?
    have these the commitment of management?

Are training needs assessed on the basis of:
    manpower forecasts?
    job analysis?
    performance reviews?

Are training plans prepared setting out:
    problem areas?
    proposed action?
    responsibility for action?
    costs of the proposals?
    future benefits?

Are the training needs of each of the main categories of employees adequately catered for by the training plan and the existing training schemes? Are these flexible?

With regard to internal training programmes and courses:
    are these based on a proper assessment of collective and individual training needs?

    are the overall objectives of courses clearly defined, if possible in terms of standards of performance to be attained?

    is the syllabus logically planned and properly related to the overall objectives?

    are the individuals responsible for the training properly trained — and effective in conducting the courses?

    do the programmes consist of a balanced mix of formal instruction, discussion, projects, case studies and practice as appropriate?

    are adequate steps taken to follow-up after training to ensure that what has been taught is effectively being put into practice?

are training programmes evaluated and modified in the light of the follow-up action?

Are external courses selected carefully on the basis of assessments of:
individual training needs?
the relevance and value of the course in relation to the training needs?

Is follow-up action taken to assess the value of the course to the individual and the organisation?

Can external consultants/speakers be used within the internal training programme?

What involvement is there with the Government Training Board?

Are there any committees within the industry service that can offer advice on training matters?

Can tailored individual external courses be used to supplement internal and ordinary external training?

Do:

regard him as a challenge to existing management skills
set him clear objectives and aggressive deadlines
make time to discuss his ideas and suggestions
challenge his ideas and be constructively critical
treat him as a valued member of his team
be quick to praise him for outstanding achievement
see that his salary increases reflect his extra contribution
ask for his suggestions and ideas on some of the existing problems
nominate him for courses which would assist his development
request only those reports which are required

Do not:

allow him to be viewed as a threat to other peoples security
leave him to guess what he is expected to achieve
always be 'too busy' to see him
display indifference or be negative and carping
make him constantly aware of senior status
ignore his achievements (or allow his credits to be stolen)
reward him exactly the same as everyone else
be excessively secretive or discourage his interest
deny him opportunities in case he should appear more knowledgeable than you
keep badgering for reports which you promptly file

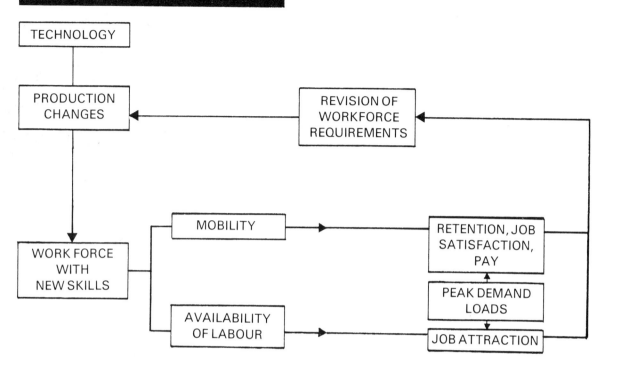

What attracts employees away from an organisation?:

high earnings
fringe benefits
furthering one's career
alternative job opportunities
greater job satisfaction

What pushes employees out of an organisation?:

need to avoid personal conflicts
running down of staff
induction crisis
pressures from shortage of labour
pressures from changed working requirements or conditions

Reasons for discharge:

unsuitable
disciplinary reasons
redundancy
shortage of materials
seasonal fluctuation
restricted operations

Reasons for resignation:

remuneration
hours of work
physical working conditions
dissatisfaction with job
relationship with:
    fellow workers
    supervisors
personal betterment
national service
transport difficulties
housing difficulties
domestic responsibilities
illness or accident
marriage
pregnancy
move from district
retirement
death

Organisation requirements:

the job title of the individual to whom the job holder reports
the job titles of each of the individuals reporting directly to the job holder
a summary for each immediate subordinate of the overall purpose of the job and the main functions or activities which are carried out or for which responsibility attaches
wherever possible quantitative data should be obtained on the scale of the activities of each subordinate or the section controlled by the subordinate
details of the organisation structure under each subordinate, including the number and types of staff they supervise.
(It is often only necessary to go down to the level immediately below the subordinate although there may be occasions when a fuller picture of the organisation structure is required.)

Questions designed to assess the relative importance of tasks:

what would you regard as your most important duties?
what are the duties which take up a significant proportion of your time?
which aspect of the job causes you most problems?
how in broad terms, do you find your time is being spent in a typical day, week or month?
how much time do you find you are spending:

in meetings with two or more people
in face-to-face discussions with your superior, subordinates, or colleagues with other contacts outside the company
writing reports or memoranda
thinking about plans, policies or problems

Accountability

Employees' understanding:

    are you expected to formulate your own targets or are these given to you?

    how much freedom have you to act within a given policy?

    who approves your operating plans and budgets?

    how far can you go in changing the organisation structure of your department or re-allocating duties without reference to your superior?

    on staffing matters to what extent and to what level can you:

        increase your establishment

        engage staff

        promote staff

        fix salaries on recruitment, transfer or promotion

        re-grade jobs

        award merit increments

        discipline staff

        dismiss staff

    with regard to each area of responsibility, on what matters and how often do you approach higher authority (your immediate superior or any other functional head or a committee) in order to:

        make recommendations on a course of action

        obtain approval for a proposed course of action

        seek advice on a problem

        give information on an action you have taken

    with regard to each area of responsibility, who makes the final decision on what is to be done?

    who decides what control information you produce?

    who sees the control information and how is it dealt with?

    what is your authority to spend?

Resources controlled by the job:

Obtain details of any resources controlled:

    total number of staff controlled

    annual expenditure budget (broken-down under main headings)

    details of capital expenditure

    value of assets controlled

    size and number of assets controlled, for example, floor space and locations of buildings

    volumes: throughput, items or queries processed, cases dealt with

    turnover

    profit or contribution

Find out for each of the resources controlled its size in proportion to the total resources of the organisation.

Knowledge and skills:

Information must be available on:

    any professional, technical or academic qualifications that are essential or desirable to the effective performance of the job

    the type and amount of experience required — essential or desirable

    the extent to which the job holder has to have knowledge of the procedures and systems used in the organisation

Skills required must be assessed in terms of:

    man management

    administration

    commercial activities

    contacts with other people — to inform, influence, advise or persuade

    communications — written or spoken

    the analytical requirements of the work

Decisions required by job holder:

Establish the level of decision taking involved in the job by analysing:

    the amount of authority the job holder has to take decisions

    the importance of the decisions — this can be assessed in a number of ways, for example:

the extent to which the job holder personally influences the output, turnover, profits or contribution for which he is responsible

the amount of influence exerted by the job holder on objectives and targets, corporate or functional policies, short and long range plans

the importance of the objectives, policies and plans with regard to their short and long term impact on the results achieved by the organisation, and their scope in terms of the extent to which they cover the whole or parts of the organisation

the time scale over which decisions are made — this covers the length of time over which plans or programmes are devised and the time span between taking the decision and obtaining the control information which will indicate its effectiveness

be provided by an analysis of the extent to which the jobs of immediate subordinates vary in responsibility or the activities they carry out

the number of units controlled and the differences between them

the range and variety of products which the job holder produces, markets, sells or distributes

the range and variety of equipment for which the job holder is responsible or which he uses himself

the range and variety of contacts made by the job holder inside and outside the organisation

the variety of skills used by the job holder

Difficulty of the decisions

This can be assessed by checking with regard to each area of decision:

the amount of guidance received from superiors

the existence of clearly defined procedures or precedents and the extent to which the job holder has to use judgment in using the procedures or applying the precedents

any problems in obtaining the information required to take the decisions

any problems in forecasting the outcome of decisions

the amount of original thinking or creativity required to solve problems

Job complexity

The complexity of the job should be assessed by obtaining information on:

the number or range of different functions or activities controlled — a lead on this should

The main types of performance assessment are:

overall assessment
guideline assessment
grading
merit rating
critical incident
target setting

Performance appraisal:

If there exists a systematic performance appraisal procedure, has the method any of the following weaknesses where:

managers assess undefined personality traits rather than comparing actual performance against agreed standards and targets
employees are unaware of the results of the performance review except as it affects their salary increments
managers do not attempt to hold counselling meetings with their staff to discuss strengths and weaknesses and agree training and development needs
performance review reports are not used to identify training and development needs or to establish potential for promotion
the system is over-elaborate

Assessing Potential:

has the employee been long enough in his present job to form an assessment?
what are the employee's views about the present job?
in the light of the answers to the above questions, how long should the employee continue in the present job?
what sort of things can the employee do well?
what sort of things is the employee less good at?
what are the employee's interests and ambitions?
what jobs could the employee move to, in the short and longer term?
what further training and experience does the employee require before promotion?
can the employee get the training and experience required in the present job or have special arrangements to be made?

The choice of approach will depend on a number of considerations, the main ones being:

the size and complexity of the organisation
the type of jobs to be covered
the type of organisation and its management style
the climate of industrial and employee relations
equal pay
cost
time and resources available
the general pay situation

Methods used to determine salary levels, e.g.:

no formal method
job evaluation

If no formal method is used, what influences decisions on salary levels:

nationally negotiated salary changes
movements in the cost of living
movements in market rates
pressures from staff unions
pressures from increases in hourly paid workers' rates or earnings

If a system of job evaluation is used:

is it non-analytical (e.g. whole job ranking) or analytical (e.g. factor comparison)?

if non-analytical:
is ranking based on detailed job descriptions and comparisons with bench mark jobs?
are paired comparisons used to rank jobs?

if analytical:
do the factors represent significant criteria for comparing the jobs?
do the factors overlap?

is the system understood and accepted by employees?
is the system cost-effective in the sense that it is simple to maintain and not over-elaborate in relation to the accuracy of the results achieved?
have the staff administering the system been properly trained in its use?

are regular surveys carried out to compare market rates?

has the organisation a policy on where its salary and wage levels should be in relation to market rates?

how do salary and wage levels compare with market rates — locally and nationally?

how do fringe benefits compare with those provided elsewhere?

are individuals progressed through job grades and promoted on the basis of formal assessments of performance and potential?

Which way was the scheme introduced?

was it specially developed within the organisation?

was it a proprietary brand introduced with the help of consultants?

was it a scheme taken from the shelf without any attempt being made to adapt it to the needs of the organisation?

Schemes developed or introduced with the help of consultants:

check on the use of bench-mark jobs:
was the sample large enough?
was the samply fully representative?
did the sample include jobs which would facilitate both internal and external comparisons?
check on the methods used to analyse jobs:
was the analysis confined to existing job descriptions? — if so, how adequate were they for this purpose?
were job holders required to complete questionnaires and how effectively were they completed?
were job holders interviewed — if so, were check lists used which ensured that all points were covered, and was the information obtained from job holders confirmed by the superiors?
check on the job descriptions:
are they clearly divided into sections covering the overall purpose of the job, the organisational relationships of the job holder, the main activities carried out, and an analysis, where applicable,

of the job in terms of the factors used in evaluation scheme?

does the description of the overall purpose of the job clearly convey in one or two sentences the main function or role of the job holder in a way which distinguishes the job from others?

does the description identify the job title of the individual to whom the job holder is responsible and the job titles of all the individuals directly responsible to him?

are the separate activities clearly defined?

does the description of each activity convey adequately what is done without the use of unnecessary verbiage or vague adjectives?

are quantitative examples given where relevant?

does the job description adequately convey the level of authority exercised by the job holder, the amount of direction and guidance received from line or functional superiors, the relationships maintained within and outside the organisation, the complexity of the job and the knowledge and skills that are required to do it?

are the resources controlled by the job holder adequately defined?
check on the competence of those who developed the scheme:
what was their prior experience?
what training have they received?

Job ranking, as a means to evaluation:

were rank orders established by paired comparisons?
was a team of trained judges used to rank the jobs?
how were the jobs slotted into grades?

A job classification type scheme:

were the grades defined on the basis of a job analysis and job ranking exercise?
is the hierarchy of levels of responsibility clearly defined by the descriptions so that

successive levels can easily be distinguished from one another?

are the broad grade definitions supplemented by cross references to examples drawn from bench-mark jobs?

how helpful are the grade definitions in deciding on the grading of jobs in border line cases?

A points type scheme:

are there so many factors that the scheme appears to be unnecessarily complicated?

are the factors appropriate for the jobs covered by the scheme and do they cover the key areas common to all jobs without too much overlap?

are the factors and the levels within the factors adequately defined?

was the weighting of the factors decided on an arbitrary basis or was a special exercise such as multiple regression analysis used to calculate weightings?

could an equally acceptable result be obtained by using a simpler approach such as job classification, supported by market surveys?

were staff given adequate information about the scheme during its development and have they been kept informed subsequently?

Basic features:

entry age for membership

contributions

pension on retirement

cash options on retirement

late retirement

post-retirement pension increases

widows/widowers benefits

early retirement

early leavers

'top hat' arrangements

integration with state provisions

funding

Present arrangements:

The following information should be obtained about the existing pension scheme or schemes:

whether the scheme is self-administered or insured (and in the latter case the annual renewal date)

the total membership of the scheme or schemes

the total scheme salary roll or a list of individual scheme salaries

numbers not included in the schemes and the reasons why

eligibility for membership of the scheme or schemes (is it compulsory?)

entry requirements — minimum and maximum age on entry for men and women

whether the scheme(s) is contributory or non-contributory, and if contributory the scale of contributions

the retirement ages for males and females

the retirement formula and scale of benefits on retirement, for example:

final salary (salary service) — the pension fraction (n/60ths etc.), number years that can count as pensionable service and basis for determining final salary (e.g. average of last three years' salary):

total earnings (average salary) — the ratio of pension to the mean scheme salary in each class (1 per cent or 1½ per cent etc.) and the relationship between pensionable earnings and actual earnings; flat rate or money purchase;

lump sum option (commutation rights) — availability of option, the amount that can be obtained and the basis for calculating the amount

late retirement — the provisions for improving the pension if the employee works on after normal retiring date and the formula used, if any, to determine the improvement

pension increases — the provisions, if any, for relating increases to a cost of living index or a pre-determined percentage figure, such as 3 per cent compound a year

widows' pensions and lump sum provisions after death in service

widows' pensions after death in retirement — whether commencing immediately on death or following a guaranteed period of payment of the member's pension

early retirement pension provisions

early leavers — arrangements for:
    returning contributions
    freezing rights to accrued benefit
    transferring accrued benefits to new employer

top hat scheme — provisions for providing individuals with a greater pension benefit than that given by the main fund

salary sacrifice — provisions for allowing staff to sacrifice part of their salary to gain an enhanced pension (maximum benefits are however related to the reduced salary)

the basis upon which pensionable earnings calculated — are bonuses, commission, overtime or other emoluments included and if so, is an average of previous years, usually three, taken

integration — whether or not the scheme is integrated (i.e. takes account of the State flat rate pension) and if it is, the method of integration, for example:
    full integration
    'salary disregard'
    lower fraction throughout
    variable fractions

The steps to take when introducing or amending a pension scheme are as follows:

analyse present arrangements

make a preliminary assessment of the need to change present arrangements and select advisers to help in developing the new or revised scheme

identify and evaluate the alternative arrangements for each aspect of the pension scheme from the point of view of:
    the requirements of the Revenue code of approval
    latest legislation
    costs
    funding and administration

consider in the light of the information obtained from the analysis above the case for making the scheme contributory or non-contributory and the level of contributions required

consult staff

make a preliminary decision on:
    the range and level of benefits that should be provided
    contribution arrangements
    funding and administrative arrangements

prepare a clear and easy to read summary of the proposed arrangements for discussion with staff

make any final modifications to the scheme in the light of the views of the staff

issue a provisional notification of the scheme to staff

obtain approval from the Inland Revenue

complete all administrative arrangements with the trustees and, where appropriate, the insurance company

ensure that a concise, informative and readable booklet is prepared for the staff

communicate details of the new scheme to staff — be prepared to allow time for discussions with individual members of staff on how the scheme affects them

See Also:

7 Finance and Accounting

Short-term:
Up to one year
    bank overdrafts
    bill financing
    supplier credit
    invoice discounting
    credit factoring

Medium-term:
One to five years
    hire purchase
    deferred instalment
    equipment leasing
    term loans

Long-term:
Over five years

    long-term loans
    investors — ordinary shares
            — preference shares
            — undistributed profits (reserves)
    debenture or similar loan stock

A Balance Sheet is a summary of . . . . ASSETS and LIABILITIES

ASSETS are generally classified into . . . . FIXED ASSETS and CURRENT ASSETS

FIXED ASSETS consist of . . . . TANGIBLE ASSETS Property
                                                         Plant & Machinery
                                                         Motor Vehicles

                                         INTANGIBLE ASSETS Goodwill
                                                         Patents

FIXED ASSETS can be valued at . . . . Cost
Cost less depreciation
Valuation
Replacement Value
(or a combination of each)

CURRENT ASSETS can be valued at . . . . Realisable amount (e.g. expectation of amount receivable from debtors after reserving for possible bad debts)
Cost, including an amount for the value of work in progress (i.e. in the case of stock)

LIABILITIES are stated at . . . . The monetary amount necessary to discharge the indebtedness

---

It is essential when a balance sheet is used as the basis of calculations for:
    Net Worth or Net Value
    Return on Capital
    Fixed v Current Investment
    Ratio comparison
    Borrowings (i.e. gearing)
    Insurance

that the method used to arrive at asset values is identified and stated

FIXED ASSETS should be financed by Permanent or Long-Term sources of Capital
CURRENT ASSETS should be financed from Short term sources (creditors, overdrafts etc.)

Stylised Balance Sheet in 7.3 shows this by example

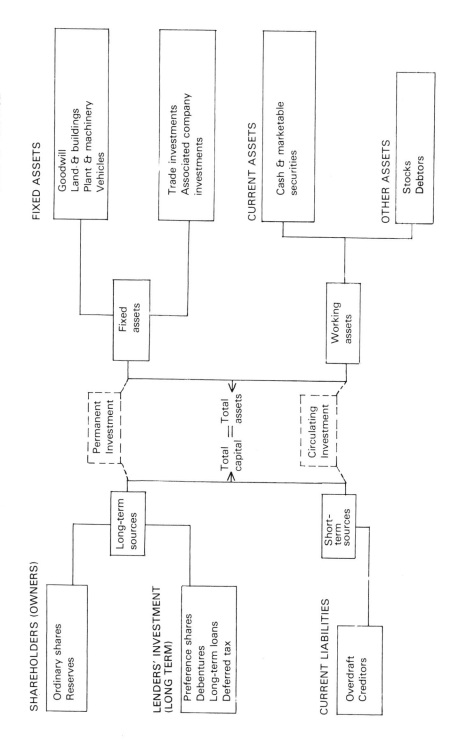

SOURCE OF FINANCE

USES OF FINANCE

SHAREHOLDERS' (OWNERS)

Ordinary shares
Reserves

LENDERS' INVESTMENT
(LONG TERM)

Preference shares
Debentures
Long-term loans
Deferred tax

CURRENT LIABILITIES

Overdraft
Creditors

Long-term
sources

Short-
term
sources

Permanent
Investment

Circulating
Investment

Total $=$ Total
capital   assets

Fixed
assets

Working
assets

FIXED ASSETS

Goodwill
Land & buildings
Plant & machinery
Vehicles

Trade investments
Associated company
investments

CURRENT ASSETS

Cash & marketable
securities

OTHER ASSETS

Stocks
Debtors

FIXED ASSETS

— Property investment:

Ascertain Cost and/or Valuation amounts (Source: Balance Sheet, Notes to Balance Sheet and Directors Report as shown in the annual accounts)

Age of freehold properties or leasehold properties.

Date of Valuation

Basis of Valuation

Realisable Value

Alternative investment, e.g. sale and lease back

Policy relating to depreciation, rate of write-off by classification of type of building or structure

Value of unexpired lease

— Plant, Machinery and Vehicles:

Type of plant, location. Value to business

Depreciation policy and adequacy in inflationary periods

Obsolescence of processes, changes in technology

Replacement cost and availability of alternative equipment

— Goodwill:

Is value justified and does it represent value of super profits? (the profits in excess of an acheivable return for the type of business)

What is the write-off policy?

CURRENT ASSETS

— Stock and work in Progress:

What indication is given regarding basis of value e.g. inclusion of overheads?

How consistent is the valuation policy?

Is the industry in a fast moving consumer sector — rate of depreciation of product lines

— Debtors:

Adequacy of provision for bad debts

Length of credit given and currency in which receivable

CONTINGENT LIABILITIES

Determine the basis of valuation in hire purchase transactions and Long-Term contracts. Also amount of contingent liabilities which could materialise into actual liability and the possible effect on liquidity

7.5 PRINCIPAL MANAGEMENT RATIOS

Markets:

- growth of sales
- growth of market share
- length of order book/sales
- debtors/sales

Capital:

- net profit after tax/shareholders' funds
- price/earnings ratio
- interest paid/borrowed capital
- total profit/interest paid
- borrowed capital/equity capital
- earnings per share
- dividend paid/market value
- dividend paid/attributable profit

Suppliers:

- suppliers' prices index
- suppliers' lead time
- days orders overdue
- creditors/purchases
- cash, debtors, marketable securities/current liabilities
- value of goods returned or credited
- purchases

Employees:

- number of leavers/average numbers employed
- average age of senior staff: now/five years ago
- 'output' per employee

Assets:

- net profit before tax to total assets
- net profit before tax to net assets
- current assets/current liabilities
- liquid assets/current liabilities
- actual output/maximum output

7.6 PRINCIPAL VARIATIONS OF RETURN ON CAPITAL CONCEPT

Ratios	Capital base	Profit base
1 Return on Total Assets	Total Assets	Net Profit before all interest charges and taxation
2 Return on Total Tangible Assets	Total Assets but excluding intangibles e.g. Goodwill, Patents etc.	As for ratio (1)
3 Return on Total Operating Assets	Total Assets but excluding intangibles and investments	As for ratio (1) but excluding investment income
4 Return on Net Assets	Total Assets less current liabilities	As for ratio (3)
5 Return on Net Tangible Assets	Total tangible assets less current liabilities	As for ratio (1)
6 Return on Net Operating Assets	Total operating assets less current liabilities	As for ratio (3)
7 Return on Long Term Capital Employed	Capital + Reserves (Total or net of intangibles) + Deferred Tax + Borrowing (Total or long term only) + Minority interests	Net profit before interest and before and after taxation
8 Return on Shareholders' funds	Capital + Reserves (Intangibles must be included)	Net profit after charging all interest and taxation and adjusting for minority interests
9 Return to holders of Ordinary shares	Issued Ordinary Capital + Reserves	As for ratio (8) but after Preference Dividends
10 Earnings Yield (at par value of shares)	Issued Ordinary Capital	As for ratio (9)
11 Earnings per share	Number of Ordinary shares in issue	As for ratio (9)

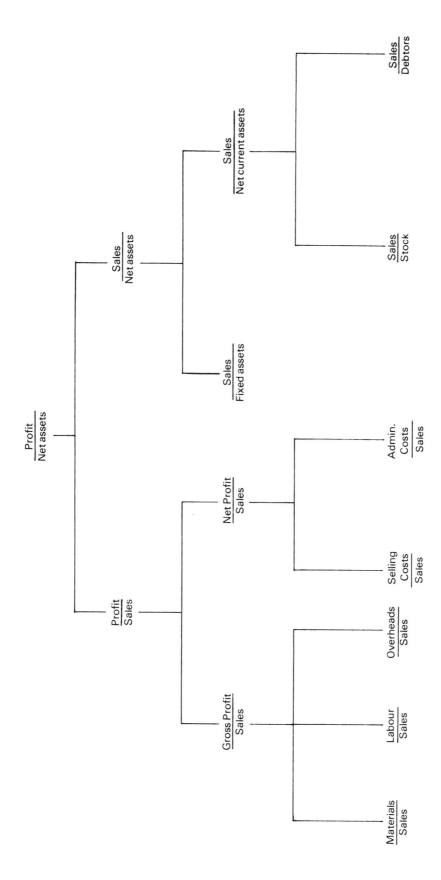

All ratios to be stated in percentages

7.8 GEARING, CASH AND WORKING CAPITAL RATIOS

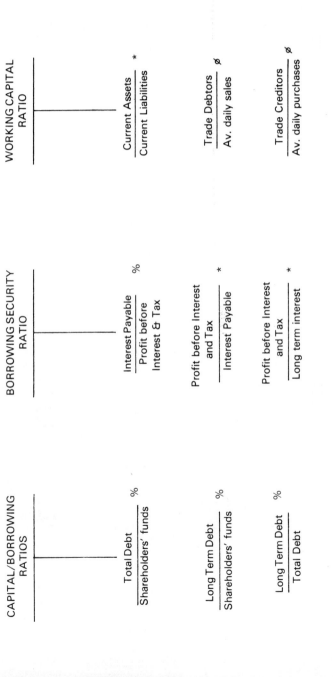

CAPITAL/BORROWING RATIOS

$$\frac{\text{Total Debt}}{\text{Shareholders' funds}} \quad \%$$

$$\frac{\text{Long Term Debt}}{\text{Shareholders' funds}} \quad \%$$

$$\frac{\text{Long Term Debt}}{\text{Total Debt}} \quad \%$$

$$\frac{\text{Total Debt}}{\text{Total Assets}} \quad \%$$

BORROWING SECURITY RATIO

$$\frac{\text{Interest Payable}}{\text{Profit before Interest \& Tax}} \quad \%$$

$$\frac{\text{Profit before Interest and Tax}}{\text{Interest Payable}} \quad *$$

$$\frac{\text{Profit before Interest and Tax}}{\text{Long term interest}} \quad *$$

WORKING CAPITAL RATIO

$$\frac{\text{Current Assets}}{\text{Current Liabilities}} \quad *$$

$$\frac{\text{Trade Debtors}}{\text{Av. daily sales}} \quad \emptyset$$

$$\frac{\text{Trade Creditors}}{\text{Av. daily purchases}} \quad \emptyset$$

$$\frac{\text{Stock}}{\text{Av. daily raw material cost of sales}} \quad \emptyset$$

LIQUIDITY RATIO

$$\frac{\text{Cash + Investment}}{\text{Trade Creditors}} \quad \%$$

$$\frac{\text{Cash, Debtors and Investments}}{\text{Total current liabilities}} \quad \%$$

* number of times

ø number of days

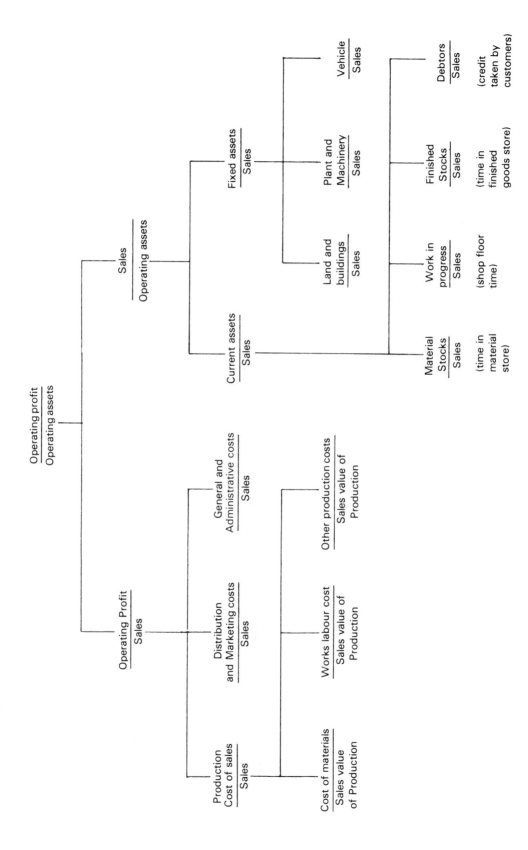

$$\frac{\text{Operating profit}}{\text{Operating assets}}$$

$$\frac{\text{Operating Profit}}{\text{Sales}}$$

$$\frac{\text{Production}}{\text{Cost of sales}} \Big/ \text{Sales}$$

$$\frac{\text{Distribution}}{\text{and Marketing costs}} \Big/ \text{Sales}$$

$$\frac{\text{General and}}{\text{Administrative costs}} \Big/ \text{Sales}$$

$$\frac{\text{Cost of materials}}{\text{Sales value of Production}}$$

$$\frac{\text{Works labour cost}}{\text{Sales value of Production}}$$

$$\frac{\text{Other production costs}}{\text{Sales value of Production}}$$

$$\frac{\text{Sales}}{\text{Operating assets}}$$

$$\frac{\text{Current assets}}{\text{Sales}}$$

$$\frac{\text{Fixed assets}}{\text{Sales}}$$

$$\frac{\text{Land and buildings}}{\text{Sales}}$$

$$\frac{\text{Plant and Machinery}}{\text{Sales}}$$

$$\frac{\text{Vehicle}}{\text{Sales}}$$

$$\frac{\text{Material Stocks}}{\text{Sales}}$$
(time in material store)

$$\frac{\text{Work in progress}}{\text{Sales}}$$
(shop floor time)

$$\frac{\text{Finished Stocks}}{\text{Sales}}$$
(time in finished goods store)

$$\frac{\text{Debtors}}{\text{Sales}}$$
(credit taken by customers)

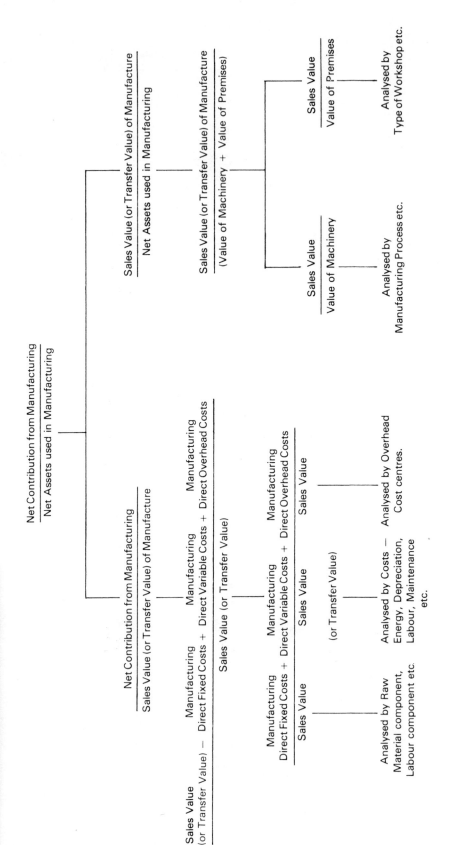

$$\frac{\text{Net Contribution from Manufacturing}}{\text{Net Assets used in Manufacturing}}$$

Left branch:

$$\frac{\text{Net Contribution from Manufacturing}}{\text{Sales Value (or Transfer Value) of Manufacture}}$$

$$= \frac{\text{Sales Value} - \text{Manufacturing} \quad \text{Manufacturing}}{(\text{or Transfer Value}) - \text{Direct Fixed Costs} + \text{Direct Variable Costs} + \text{Direct Overhead Costs}}{\text{Sales Value (or Transfer Value)}}$$

$$\frac{\text{Manufacturing}}{\text{Direct Fixed Costs} + \text{Direct Variable Costs} + \text{Direct Overhead Costs}}{\text{Sales Value}}$$

$$\frac{\text{Manufacturing}}{\text{Direct Fixed Costs}}{\text{Sales Value}}$$

Analysed by Raw Material component, Labour component etc.

$$\frac{\text{Manufacturing}}{\text{Direct Variable Costs}}{\text{Sales Value}}$$
(or Transfer Value)

Analysed by Costs — Energy, Depreciation, Labour, Maintenance etc.

$$\frac{\text{Manufacturing}}{\text{Direct Overhead Costs}}{\text{Sales Value}}$$

Analysed by Overhead Cost centres.

Right branch:

$$\frac{\text{Sales Value (or Transfer Value) of Manufacture}}{\text{Net Assets used in Manufacturing}}$$

$$\frac{\text{Sales Value (or Transfer Value) of Manufacture}}{(\text{Value of Machinery} + \text{Value of Premises})}$$

$$\frac{\text{Sales Value}}{\text{Value of Machinery}}$$

Analysed by Manufacturing Process etc.

$$\frac{\text{Sales Value}}{\text{Value of Premises}}$$

Analysed by Type of Workshop etc.

All rates to be stated in percentages

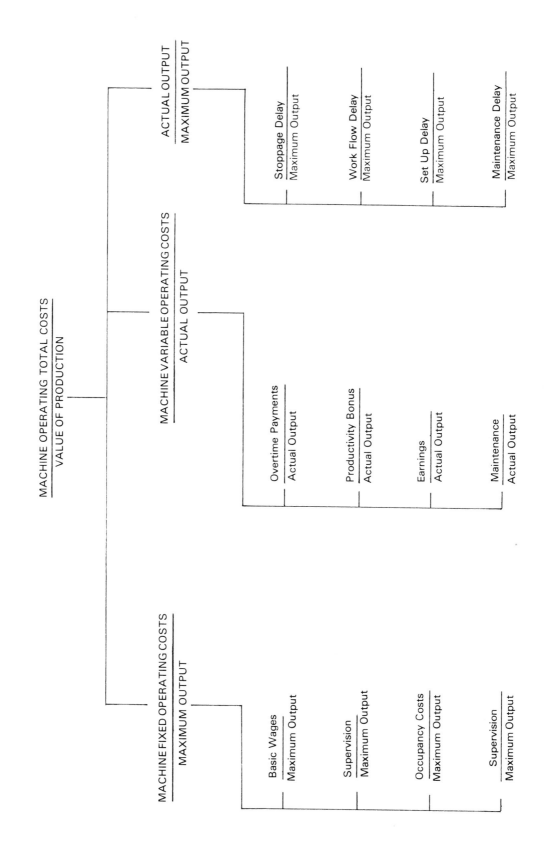

$$\frac{\text{MACHINE OPERATING TOTAL COSTS}}{\text{VALUE OF PRODUCTION}}$$

$$\frac{\text{MACHINE FIXED OPERATING COSTS}}{\text{MAXIMUM OUTPUT}}$$

$$\frac{\text{Basic Wages}}{\text{Maximum Output}}$$

$$\frac{\text{Supervision}}{\text{Maximum Output}}$$

$$\frac{\text{Occupancy Costs}}{\text{Maximum Output}}$$

$$\frac{\text{Supervision}}{\text{Maximum Output}}$$

$$\frac{\text{MACHINE VARIABLE OPERATING COSTS}}{\text{ACTUAL OUTPUT}}$$

$$\frac{\text{Overtime Payments}}{\text{Actual Output}}$$

$$\frac{\text{Productivity Bonus}}{\text{Actual Output}}$$

$$\frac{\text{Earnings}}{\text{Actual Output}}$$

$$\frac{\text{Maintenance}}{\text{Actual Output}}$$

$$\frac{\text{ACTUAL OUTPUT}}{\text{MAXIMUM OUTPUT}}$$

$$\frac{\text{Stoppage Delay}}{\text{Maximum Output}}$$

$$\frac{\text{Work Flow Delay}}{\text{Maximum Output}}$$

$$\frac{\text{Set Up Delay}}{\text{Maximum Output}}$$

$$\frac{\text{Maintenance Delay}}{\text{Maximum Output}}$$

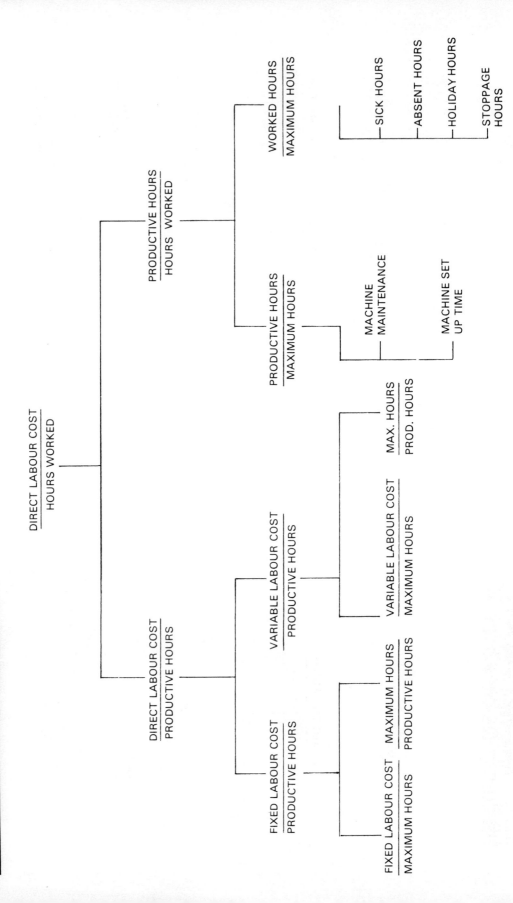

7.13 PRIORITY RATIOS FOR THE CHIEF EXECUTIVE

Areas to be considered are the relationship between a company and:

> its markets
> the providers of its capital, both risk and loan
> its suppliers
> its employees
> its trading
> its asset turnover

Market ratios:
> competitors return on capital
> competitors capital expenditure/sales
> competitors /sales
> competitors research/sales
> competitors market-share/total market

Providers of capital:
> return on shareholders' funds
> earnings yield
> dividend yield

Share price/earnings
> shareholders' funds/borrowings

Supplies:
> suppliers' return on capital
> suppliers' share of market
> suppliers' damaged or deficient supplies/purchases

Employees:
> efficiency — actual hours worked/actual production hours available
> activity — actual production hours/budgeted production hours
> capacity — actual hours worked/budgeted hours

Trading:
> gross profit/sales
> net profit/sales
> stock turnover/cost of sales
> materials/cost of production
> labour/cost of production

Production:
> production overheads/cost of production

Asset turnover:
> working capital/sales
> debtors/sales
> creditors/purchases
> fixed assets/sales
> fixed assets/working assets

Return on assets:
> ratios as for market ratios but relating to company

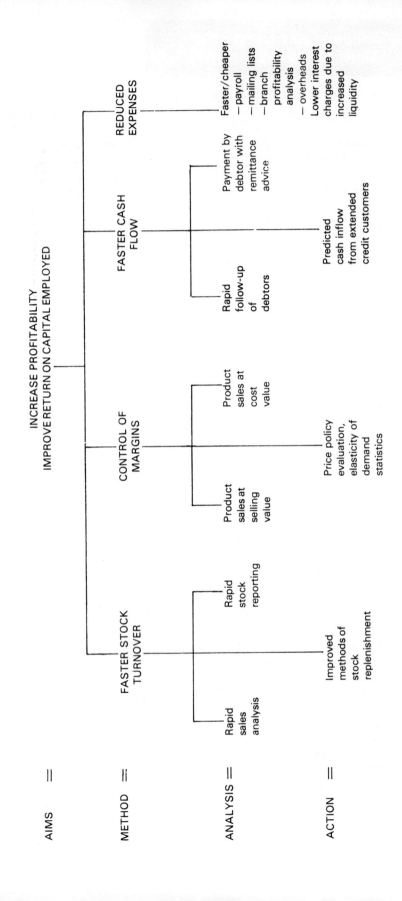

7.14 FINANCIAL OBJECTIVES OF MANAGEMENT IN RATIO TERMS

AIMS =

INCREASE PROFITABILITY
IMPROVE RETURN ON CAPITAL EMPLOYED

METHOD =

FASTER STOCK TURNOVER

CONTROL OF MARGINS

FASTER CASH FLOW

REDUCED EXPENSES

ANALYSIS =

Rapid stock reporting

Product sales at selling value

Product sales at cost value

Payment by debtor with remittance advice

Faster/cheaper
— payroll
— mailing lists
— branch profitability analysis
— overheads
Lower interest charges due to increased liquidity

Rapid sales analysis

Price policy evaluation, elasticity of demand statistics

Rapid follow-up of debtors

ACTION =

Improved methods of stock replenishment

Predicted cash inflow from extended credit customers

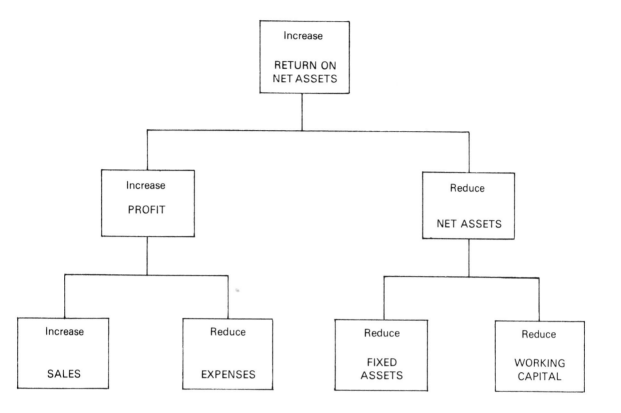

7.16 'INTERFIRM' COMPARISON OF COMPANIES

Problems of comparability:

how similar are the other firms?
how can the information be obtained?
how reliable is the information?

Comparable companies:

competitors
potential competitors
firms operating in fields the company might enter

Sources of comparison:

company accounts
trade information
trade associations
sales literature

7.17 TYPES OF REPORTS IN MANAGEMENT INFORMATION SYSTEMS

Profitability reports by:

product
division
area
customer group
channel of distribution
organisation
profit responsibility centre

Cost reports of:

labour analyses — direct labour
labour analyses — indirect labour
productive labour variances
non-productive labour variances
direct expense analysis
productivity analysis — direct labour
overtime payment analysis
analysis of spoilt work, rework and scrap
material analyses
manufacturing overhead analysis
administrative cost analysis
marketing cost analysis (order getting costs)
distribution cost analysis (order-filling costs)
product costs
cost of production
cost of sales
cost analyses for every responsibility centre
and their constituent cost centres

Sundry reports on:

orders received
orders delivered
overdue deliveries
backlog of orders at month-end
material yields
cash receipts
physical output
research and development progress report
special studies:

analysis and interpretation of problems or trends indicated by other regular reports
studies directed towards finding cost reduction opportunities

What is management accounting?

it is the interpretation of financial data for the purposes of day to day management control and decision taking

it uses the same data base as for financial accounting

it relates the present to previous plans

it is unaffected by statutory requirements relating to presentation of accounting information

it takes account of the management structure in terms of individual accountability and responsibility

it is the data recording process within the management information system

How does it operate?

budgets form a part of the management information system

actual results are compared with budgets

budgets are updated when necessary in the form of forecasts

What does a Management Accounting system include?

routine accounting statements

to show budget compared with actual profit

balance sheet

cash flow

capital expenditure

volumes manufactured and sold

performance ratios

variance statement

INPUTS	CONVERSION UNIT	OUTPUTS
capital		return on investment
labour	THE COMPANY	consumer satisfaction
materials		goods and services
services		goal attainment
knowledge		market share
plans		salary levels

The purpose of a management accounting system is:

to show the cost structure of each product and process so that effective control may be exercised

to facilitate product costing, for inventory valuation and income determination purposes

to identify profit or loss by department, process or job — this can aid in determining the output or products that will lead to the most profitable level of operations

to aid in the pricing decision by distinguishing between fixed and variable costs, thereby establishing lowest price levels

to prevent wastage by the use of an efficient system of stores and wages control

to provide cost estimate data on which to base tenders

to secure more efficient operations, and more effective use of resources, by comparison of results with pre-determined standards (variance analysis) or data supplied by similar firms

to permit the establishing of uniform cost accounting systems for inter-firm comparison purposes

to identify and permit acceptable resource allocation

to measure management accountability

to enable Accountability and Responsibility to be measured

to enable the preparation of targets, budgets and forecasts

to contribute trading over the finance information

to the preparation and interpretation of business plans

to aid long term solvency through identification of finance required

purpose of management accounting illustrated

Management accounting relates to the:

 Management Structure

 Management Information System

 Budget

 Management Accounting System

and to the interlocking

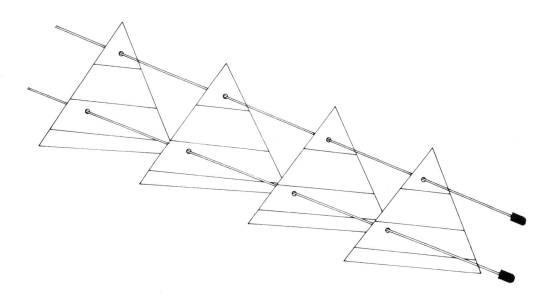

Budgeting:

> **is a management tool**
>
> is essential for short-term operational planning and control
>
> aims to anticipate change

Budgetary control system conditions depend on the following:

> management responsibility must be clear
>
> managers must see their standards and budgets as attainable
>
> the budgetary control information must be understood by those for whom it is designed
>
> training in budgetary control must be effective
>
> the organisation of information production must be appropriate
>
> managers must understand the purposes of the budgetary system

Budgets translate plans into firm parameters in terms of resource generation and utilisation in all areas against which performance can be continually monitored. Budgets can be for any period and cover the main operating areas, e.g.:

> trading statements in detail
>
> asset investment and their movement
> > fixed assets including buildings, machinery etc.
> > stocks and work in progress
> > debtors
> > total assets
>
> sales, orders received and orders on hand
> manpower
> > direct and indirect by function
> > direct and indirect by product
> > direct and indirect by division

remuneration
> direct and indirect by function
> budget for standard hours available

stock analysis
> by category (e.g. pre-process, work in progress and finished goods)
> labour input
> material input
> write-down and other provisions

expense classification
> remuneration
> commissions
> purchased services
> insurance
> depreciation

gross margin analysis by products

expense analysis by function and category
> production
> marketing
> engineering

capital expenditure by project
sales analysis by class of customer and product
analysis of floor space
analysis of reserves
balance sheet
cash flow
analysis of research and development projects
manufacturing shop loading and manpower utilisation

7.21 BUDGETARY CONTROL PROCEDURE

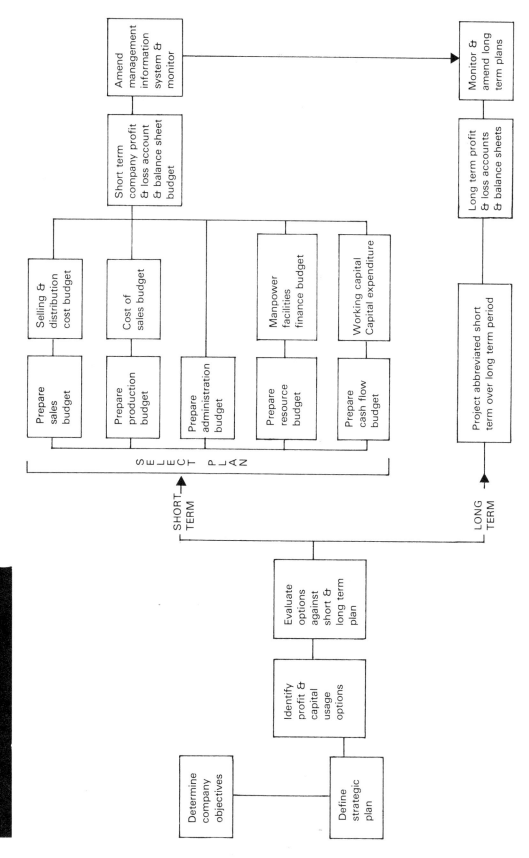

7.22 WEAKNESSES OF BUDGETARY CONTROL

Major problem areas are frequently encountered in the use of budget systems:

they can grow to be so complex, detailed, cumbersome, meaningless and expensive that they become dangerous

budgetary goals may come to supercede organisational goals, requiring care in using budgets as a *means* and not an *end*

budgets tend to hide inefficiencies — provision must be made for re-examination of standards and other bases of planning, by which policies are translated into numerical terms

the use of budgets as punitive or pressure devices defeats their basic purpose

management accountants accept standard rules of thumb without questioning the principles on which they are based and the aims in view

other functional managers have too little understanding of the methods by which costs are calculated and cannot deal with cost allocation arguments

there is a poor reconciliation process with financial accounts

7.23 FORECASTING

Forecasting is an integral part of budgeting
The design of an information system must be based on:

what information should be provided?
in what form should this information be supplied?
to whom should this information be made available?

Actual results should be related to a yardstick of performance — a predetermined plan, budget, or standard. Management information must observe important features of any control system:

accountability
controllability
selectivity

The information used must be:
impartial
valid
reliable
consistent

Good management accounting systems are based upon the following criteria:

the accurate identification of changing costs in products, product groups, markets, key customers, operations and processes

the control of these costs when they are rising, particularly within material usage and in distribution

the provision of information for effective management decisions

A bad management accounting reporting sytem can be detected from these deficiencies:

it does not react to cost inflation quickly enough

a simple costing practice which suited the business when it was small and simple, is no longer sufficient when it is large and complex

a system based upon the extrapolation of historical costs becomes badly distorted during inflation

Does the budgeting process have top management sponsorship and support?

Is the budgeting process seen as being a major tool of management rather than an accounting technique?

Can responsible individuals throughout the organisation work to budgets?

Is management by objectives (MBO) practised? — if so, do managers meet their objectives and if not, why not?

Are the figures in budget compiled on the basis of the same definitions as the actual figures with which they will be compared?

Does the budgeting process encourage delegation?

Do budgets motivate people in the desired direction?

Do all employees — and especially supervisors and managers — fully understand the cost implications of their work and are they able to plan cost expectations accordingly?

Do the budget targets lead to objective attainment?

Do the budget targets represent reasonably attainable goals?

Are budgets flexible in relation to changing conditions?

Is the budget used as a tool for co-operative planning and control rather than as an inflexible tool of dominance?

Is balance achieved between budgeting for short-run operations and planning long-term strategy?

Are plans explicit?

Are plans understood?

Are plans capable of being adapted to meet change?

Who will be affected by future plans and how will these people be affected?

Are plans (and objectives) compatible with internal and external constraints?

Are plans capable of being monitored (i.e. in quantified format)?

Is the company's level of activity expanding or contracting?

What effect does the answer to the preceding question have on:

    manpower requirements?
    financial requirements?
    administrative requirements?

Is the time period covered by the budget related to the necessity for, and the possibility of, effective management action?

Had consideration been given to adopting rolling budgeting as opposed to purely periodic budgeting?

Is the budget built on a thorough knowledge of cost behaviour patterns?

Are budgeted expenditures classified in sufficient detail and over sufficient headings to permit the estimating of costs by each major item and function under each area of responsibility?

Do budget control reports include reasons as well as results?

Is control effort focused on significant deviations from plan only?

Are responsible individuals able to help in developing cost targets for themselves and their subordinates?

Are tomorrow's winners (i.e. new products) being developed? — if so, have consumer requirements been carefully evaluated?

Is consideration being given to the use of new materials, new processes, and new technology?

Is the staff function in the budgeting process carefully distinguished from the lone function?

Is budgeting part of the duties of the management accountant? — if not, why not and if so, are his terms of reference widely known?

Does the company have a budget committee?

Are forecasting procedures adequately developed?

Is the whole planning/budgeting endeavour based on a careful and continuing evaluation of all major factors (both external and internal) that will affect the future?

Is imagination used in identifying other courses of action prior to their evaluation in relation to corporate objectives?

Can it be eliminated without much harm to the results?

Does it cost more than it is worth?

Can it be reduced in scope and cost?

Does it do more than is required?

Can it be done more cheaply another way?

Can it be done more cheaply by someone else?

Is there an alternative service from outside which is adequate but cheaper?

Can the service or expenses supporting the operation be reduced?

On a management judgement basis, can the operation be sensibly considered to provide its full share of overhead and net profit contribution?

How does it affect other costs in the business?

If you were to start the business again would you include it?

Research and Development	Manufacturing	Marketing	Distribution	Administration

Salaries:
  executives
  technical
  clerical/secretar-
    ial staff
  hourly paid
Expenses:
  travelling
  motor
  entertaining
  other
Laboratory:
  services
  consultants' fees
  safety costs
  cleaning
  maintenance
  hire of equipment
  consumable items
  sundry materials
  samples
General:
  patent cost
  trademark costs
  (royalties re-
    ceivable)
  subscriptions
  training costs
  telephone & telex
  insurances
  rent and rates
  deprecation of
    equipment
	Salaries:
	  executives
	  clerical/secretar-
	    ial staff
	  hourly paid
	Expenses:
	  travelling
	  motor
	  entertaining
	  other
	Departmental ex-
	  penses:
	  progress
	  goods inwards
	  time-keeping
	  tool room
	  production control
	  purchasing
	  personnel
	  drawing office
	  maintenance
	  quality control
	General:
	  training costs
	  services: e.g.
	    boilerhouse
	    waste disposal
	  heat, light, power
	  insurances
	  rent and rates
	  protective cloth-
	    ing
	  fire & safety
	    equipment
	  security
	  laundering
	  cleaning
	  sundry materials
	  scrap
	  telephone & telex
	  canteen expenses
	  subscriptions
	  hire of machinery
	  depreciation of
	    machinery
		Salaries:
		  executives
		  representatives
		  clerical/secretar-
		    ial staff
		Commission:
		  executives
		  representatives
		  agents
		  royalties payable
		Expenses:
		  travelling
		  motor
		  entertaining
		  other
		Office expenses:
		  stationery
		  telephone & telex
		  postages
		  cleaning
		  hire of equipment
		  maintenance of
		    equipment
		  depreciation of
		    equipment
		General expenses:
		  training costs
		  recruitment
		  subscriptions
		  hire of premises
		  maintenance
		  amortization
		  bad debts
		  legal expenses
		  discounts given
		  insurances
		  sales administra-
		    tion
		Promotion expenses:
		  sales samples
		  catalogues/price
		    lists
		  advertising agency
		    fees
		  media costs
		  production costs
		  PR fees and
		    expenses
		Marketing research:
		  agency fees
		  data processing
		    charges
		  subscriptions
			Salaries:
			  executives
			  clerical/secretar-
			    ial staff
			  hourly paid
			Expenses:
			  travelling
			  motor
			  entertaining
			  other
			Transport:
			  fleet supervision
			  road fund tax
			  insurances
			  painting &
			    lettering
			  garage expenses
			  vehicle running
			    costs
			  vehicle maintenance
			    costs
			  vehicle hire charges
			  depreciation
			Warehousing:
			  rates and rent
			  insurances
			  hire of equipment
			  maintenance of
			    equipment
			  depreciation of
			    equipment
			  stocktaking costs
			Despatch:
			  packing and
			    packaging
			  sundry materials
			  carriage outwards
			  insurances
			  maintenance of
			    equipment
			  depreciation of
			    equipment
			General:
			  canteen expenses
			  telephone & telex
			  training costs
			  heat, light, power
				Salaries:
				  directors
				  executives
				  clerical/secretarial
				    staff
				  temporary staff
				Expenses:
				  travelling
				  motor
				  entertaining
				  other
				Office expenses:
				  stationery
				  telephone & telex
				  postages
				  mailroom/reception
				  cleaning
				  hire of equipment
				  maintenance of
				    equipment
				  depreciation of
				    equipment
				EDP expenses:
				  data preparation
				  operating costs
				  systems and pro-
				    gramming
				  stationery
				  depreciation of
				    equipment
				Financial expenses:
				  audit fees
				  bank charges
				  interest payable
				  director's fees
				  superannuation
				  secretarial/
				    registrar
				  insurances
				General Expenses:
				  training costs
				  heat, light, power
				  subscriptions and
				    donations
				  security
				  personnel and
				    welfare
				  canteen expenses
				  legal and other
				    charges
				  hire of premises
				  rates
				  maintenance

TYPE	BASIS OF ALLOCATION
Waiting time	On the one hand, productive man-hours for total productive tasks (whether for sale or for stock); on the other, productive man-hours available from the existing work force after absenteeism and overtime
Work Shop cleaning	If done as a full-time job, probably determined by floor area of factory
Training time	Number of productive workers and rate of labour turnover
Supervision	Number of productive workers
Inspection	When method of inspection has been fixed, number and mix of units produced
Storekeeping and buying	When stock-holding policy has been established, number and mix of units produced
Shop clerical work	Number of productive workers and size of productive workers and size of production batches
Payroll department	Total number of people employed — productive and indirect
Graduated pension contributions	Total gross pay
Power costs	Machine-hours run
Heating and lighting	Floor area or cubic area affected
Rent and rates for premises	In the short run, fixed; in the longer run, determined by total personnel employed, machines installed and required holdings of stock and work in progress — probably rationalised as product volume and mix
Machine lubricants	Machine-hours run
Consumable tools	Production hours, or units produced
Consumable materials	Units produced
Insurance	Valuation of buildings, or stocks or total payroll — dependent on risk insured

Three broad categories:

Blanket Method:
> Where all expenses to be allocated are lumped together and charged to cost centres on some predetermined ratio of unit activity to total company or group activity. The bases used more commonly are total expenses; payroll; cost of sales; sales; cost of investment or return on investment.

Individual Method:
> Where each category of expense to be allocated is charged out on an individual basis.
> The bases used include data processing to number of computer hours, legal expenses to direct staff hours and personnel department expenses to the recipient unit employee numbers.

Combination Method:
> Where certain identifiable expenses are charged out to cost centres on an individual basis; the remaining expenses distributed on the blanket basis.

Advantages and Disadvantages

Blanket Method:
> Relatively simple to administer
> Avoids distortions in charge out
> Easily understood
> Encourages economies in charge out base e.g. capital employed
> Charge out bears little relationship to service performed
> Charge out is arbitrary

Individual Method:
> Correspond more closely to actual services provided
> Less emotive to managers
> Overspending can be related to individual's responsibility
> Considerable administrative effort involved
> Charge outs give an impression of accuracy

Combination Method:
> Permits allocation of costs on a more identifiable basis
> More closely represents the actual situation; Imparts feeling of fairness
> Necessitates greater administrative and accounting effort

Guidelines relating to any cost allocation formula:

> the allocation basis must be seen to be effective and equitable;
> managers must be aware of the formula used;
> managers must be encouraged to question allocated costs;
> managers must be encouraged to reduce allocated cost by effectively altering the base under their control e.g. numbers employed;
> the allocation must be adhered to in such a manner as will influence decision-taking

Marginal costing v. absorption costing.

Advantages of marginal costs procedures:

marginal costing systems are simple to operate, they do not involve the problems of overhead apportionments and recovery

marginal costing avoids the difficulties of having to explain the purpose and basis of overhead absorption. Fluctuations in profit are easier to explain because they result from cost-volume interactions and not from changes in inventory

marginal costing introduces a direct relationship between sales volume and marginal income (i.e. the contribution).

marginal costing shows which products are making a contribution and which are failing to cover their avoidable (i.e. variable) costs

Disadvantages of marginal costs procedures:

economic selling prices over the long run cannot be set without some attention being paid to fixed costs. Each product line/job must not just cover its marginal costs, but collectively the contributions of all jobs must cover at least all costs if a profit is to be made

the importance of time tends to be overlooked in marginal costing: two jobs may have the same marginal cost, but one may take twice as long to complete as the other and hence its 'true' cost will be more

the difficulties and dangers of spreading fixed overhead costs do not mean that they should be ignored: they are just as vital as are direct wage costs, etc. in fact, as production becomes more automated and greater in volume, more costs will tend to be fixed, and hence they should not be overlooked

Factors which will determine the use of absorption costing or marginal costing will be:

the system of financial control in use (e.g. responsibility accounting is inconsistent with absorption costing).

the production methods in use (e.g. marginal costing is favoured in simple processing situations in which all products receive similar attention; but when different products receive widely differing amounts of attention, then absorption costing may be more realistic)

the significance of the prevailing level of fixed overhead costs

A system of marginal costing should detect:

a change in either the selling price of a product or its variable cost rate will alter the break-even point and the contribution margin ratio (i.e. the proportion of sales revenue that is left when variable cost is deducted).

when sales are above the break-even point, a high contribution margin ratio will result in greater profits than will a small contribution margin ratio

a low contribution margin ratio will require a large increase in sales volume to create a significant increase in profit

if other factors stay constant, a change in total fixed costs will alter the break-even point by the same percentage and the net profit will vary by the same amount as the change in total fixed costs

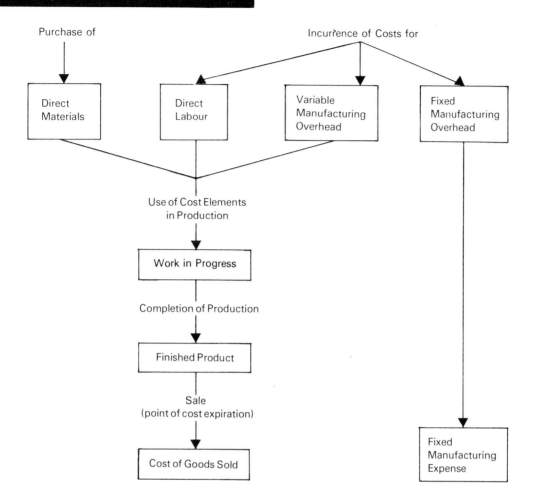

7.31 FLOW OF MANUFACTURING COSTS IN ABSORPTION COSTING

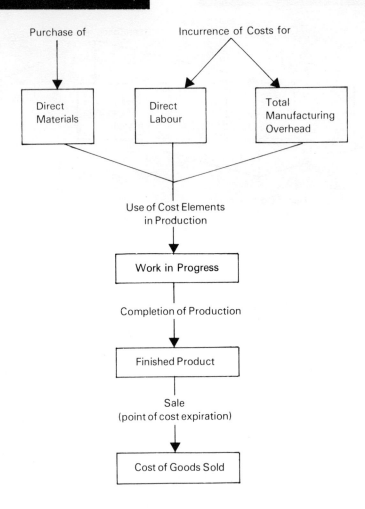

Is the company's costing system tailored to the company's needs?

Have cost centres been clearly defined?

Are the benefits of the system commensurate with its costs?

Are all costs classified into their direct and indirect, fixed and variable, controllable and uncontrollable, and separate and joint categories?

Is the behaviour of different costs understood in relation to changes in the level of activity?

Are cost reports made available promptly? How often? How quickly?

Could statements be presented earlier if more estimates were used? (Are estimating procedures reliable?)

Are figures rounded so that results are more easily understood?

Can any figures of small value be grouped?

Are the descriptions of reported items clear?

Are unusual items adequately explained?

Will further (or less) mechanisation affect the overhead of cost accounting?

Can the effectiveness of cost accounting procedures be improved?

Has sufficient thought been given to the type of costing system to use? (for example, standard costing, absorption costing, or marginal costing.)

Has the purpose for which costing is being performed been fully considered? (for example, pricing, product costing, cost control)

Is the costing system adequate in determining the relative efficiencies and profitable divisions, processes, product lines, jobs?

Is the costing system adequate for the needs of EDP and operations research analysts?

Are ratios, graphs etc, used to supplement the figures produced by the costing system?

Is a satisfactory procedure being operated to price material issues from stores?

Are all withdrawals of stock and ordering of goods from outside suppliers duly authorised by requisitions?

Are job allocation numbers recorded against labour time, material usage, etc., in all cases?

Do employees understand the importance of recording the allocation of time to jobs? How are they encouraged to do this accurately?

What is the basis for the apportionment of each service departments' costs? Is the most suitable basis selected in every case?

How are overheads absorbed into productive output? Is the most suitable basis used?

What action is taken on the basis of over or under-recovery of overheads?

Are normalised over recovery rates used? If not, why not? For example, is the level of activity stable from month to month?

Have separate overhead rates been developed for fixed overhead costs and variable overhead costs?

Why are overheads absorbed (if they are absorbed)?

Is the contribution margin concept understood within the company?

Is cost-volume-profit analysis undertaken?

Is marginal costing undertaken?

Has the company's margin of safety ever been worked out?

Are the comparative advantages and disadvantages of marginal costing versus absorption costing fully appreciated?

Is the costing system closely geared to the type of production processes operated?

What role does cost accounting play in relation to special decision-making?

Does the cost control system have the active backing of top management?

Do controls conform to the organisation structures?

Is the system seen as being an essential part of the company's management process?

Are responsible individuals aware of the need to plan their activities?

Do those individuals charged with various costs really have control over these costs?

Are cost controls established according to the nature of the tasks?

Do all who require it receive cost information?

Do responsible individuals who are held accountable play a full role in setting cost levels?

Is cost control information geared to the requirements of responsible individuals?

Is the costing system adequate in general terms?

Do control reports cover both financial and related causal factors?

Are cost control requirements and reports discussed with recipients?

Does the basis of measuring desired performance reflect those aspects of output and input that are important?

Is the principle of management by exception followed?

Are results measured in accordance with the same units of measure in which the standards are set?

Do recipients of control information know how to extract the most essential facts?

Are controls flexible and economical in operation?

Are deviations reported rapidly?

Do controls help to explain variances and to indicate the corrective action that is required?

Are control reports brief, simple to read, and relevant?

Are actions taken on the basis of these reports?

Are control reports used to indicate relative efficiencies?

Do all employees understand the cost implications of their work?

Do all employees have cost targets?

Do the benefits of the cost control system outweigh its costs?

Are unnecessary reports eliminated, and are new ones introduced only when clearly needed?

Is the control system revised each time an organisational change takes place?

Do good relations exist between the accounting staff and line management?

7.34 BREAK EVEN ANALYSIS AND GRAPH

Definition:

Break-even analysis is a technique which, by means of graphic representation, endeavours to indicate clearly the relationship between a company's costs, turnover and profit.

Fields of Application:

This analysis can be applied to nearly all commercial managerial problems, such as:

What are the consequences of an intended price increase?
What are the consequences if the sales-mix is changed?
What are the consequences for the profit if the fixed and variable costs change?
At which level of turnover does the company begin to lose?
By how much can the turnover decrease before the company begins to lose?

Description:

Break-even analysis is based on cost and turnover information. This information is set out graphically. The division of the costs into fixed and variable costs is of essential importance. Fixed costs are ones which, over a set period, are not affected by any change in turnover (per unit sales); variable costs, on the other hand, are affected by the level of turnover.

Examples of fixed costs are:

Depreciation
Rent and rates
Heating (standing charge)
Telephone rentals
Fixed loan interest
Vehicle licence
Certain insurance premiums
Administrative salaries

BREAK-EVEN CHART

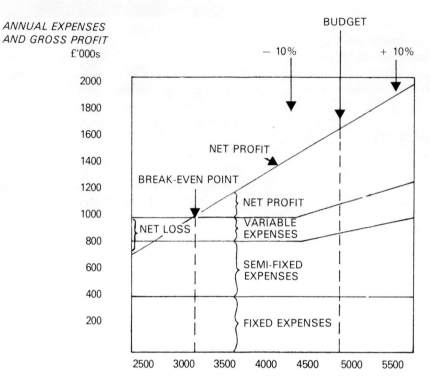

ANNUAL EXPENSES
AND GROSS PROFIT
£'000s

BUDGET

— 10%   + 10%

NET PROFIT

BREAK-EVEN POINT

NET PROFIT

NET LOSS

VARIABLE EXPENSES

SEMI-FIXED EXPENSES

FIXED EXPENSES

2000
1800
1600
1400
1200
1000
800
600
400
200

2500   3000   3500   4000   4500   5000   5500

TURNOVER - £'000s

Interpretation:

	Budget turnover (less 10%)	Budget	Budget turnover (plus 10%)
	£000's	£000's	£000s
Turnover	4366	4852	5337
Gross Margin	1445	1667	1867
Fixed Expenditure	400	400	400
Semi Fixed Expenditure	434	500	560
Variable Expenditure	235	263	288
Total Expenditure	1049	1163	1248
Net Profit	396	502	619

Profit is earned when the cash equivalent is received from the buyer. A business has many income-producing activities operating at the same time and profit or loss from any one transaction is not readily identifiable. The following example shows the time cycle for one transaction from the commencement of manufacture until the profit is realised in cash.

The example also shows how credit terms given by raw material suppliers (including manual services) and that given to purchasers of the finished article affects the overall financing of the manufacturing process to the final sale and realisation of profit.

Assumptions:

CREDITORS	TOTAL COST	PRODUCTION PROCESS	WEEKLY COST	CREDIT TERMS
Raw Material	£600	8 weeks	£75	5 weeks
Wages	£200	''	£25	2 weeks (i.e. paid at end of 2nd week)
Overheads	£120	''	£15	2 weeks
Cost of manufacture	£920		£115	
DEBTORS				
Selling Price	£1,000	—	—	2 weeks

Week	Cumulative Cost of Production		Amounts owed to Creditors	Bank Account			
				Weekly Cash		Cumulative Cash	
	Wkly. £	Cum. £	Cum. £	Rec'd £	Paid £	in credit £	overdrawn £
1	115	115	115		—		—
2	115	230	190		40		40
3	115	345	265		40		80
4	115	460	340		40		120
5	115	575	415		40		160
6	115	690	415		115		275
7	115	805	415		115		390
8	115	920	415		115		505
9		920	300		115		620
10		920	225		75		695
11			150	1000	75	230	
12			75		75	155	
13					75	80	

NOTES
1. The cost of production arises evenly over period of 8 weeks to £920. Until the article is sold and paid for the £920 has to be financed.
2. The amount available from creditors (including the week 1 wages in hand) rises to a maximum of £415. This is equivalent to an interest free loan.
3. Bank overdraft rises over the period as creditors are paid. If the buyer did not pay the £1,000 until week 14 the bank overdraft would rise to £920. No allowance has been made in the example for bank interest.
4. Time span is 11 weeks from commencement of production until profit received. After paying remaining creditors final cash balance at week 13 equals profit. The same information presented graphically would be:

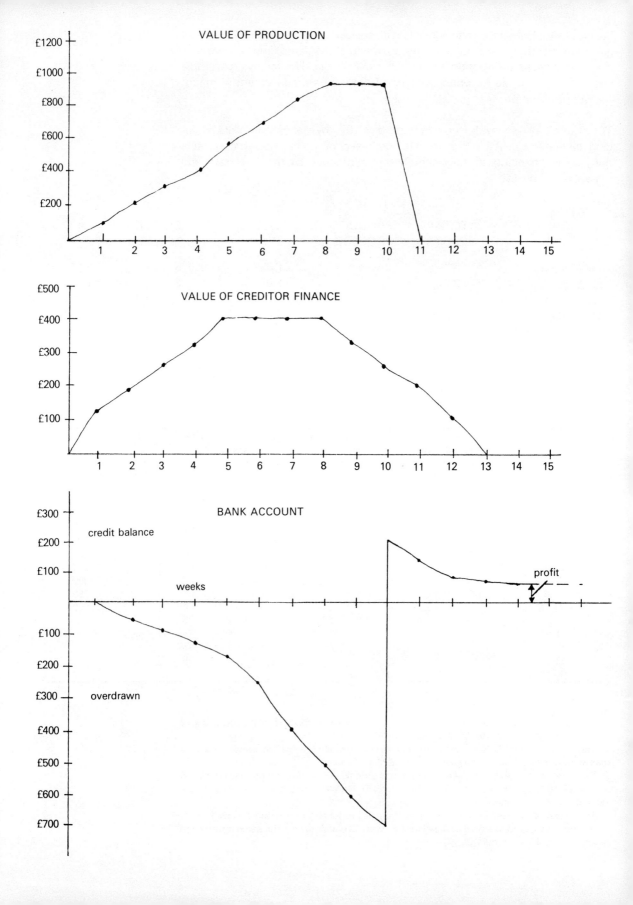

The management of cash is a vital part of every business activity — holding too few assets in the form of cash, or near cash, runs the risk of technical insolvency; holding too much, it is probably losing opportunities to earn additional revenue, thus making the whole enterprise more profitable.

Cash is both:
> an essential raw material
> a major product

Inflation has the following effects upon business:

> Increased values of credit sales require greater investment in debtors
> Markets are distorted, forcing companies to become more flexible in their operations
> Expenses rise faster than does the income from sales
> Traditional (historical cost) accounting does not show a true picture of a factual situation
> Product costing becomes difficult because of uncertainty in raw material costs
> Credit from suppliers becomes more difficult to obtain
> Suppliers pursue outstanding debts harder
> The value of stocks increases with no increase in volume sales
> Cost of new equipment escalates beyond the depreciation retention
> Loans become expensive and difficult to obtain unless backed by security

Trading in an inflationary economy means that more money is required to finance a business which has not changed the physical volume of its operations.

The capital invested in items required to support expenses prior to their re-conversion into cash after the sale of a finished product or service is termed working capital.

Working capital is circulating capital

Working capital is the investment in:
> Trade debtors (the amount owing by credit customers)
>
> Stock and work-in-progress

and financed by:
> Trade creditors (the amount owed to suppliers of materials)
>
> Bank overdrafts and short term loans

The aim is to:
> *minimise* the investment in debtors and stock and work-in-progress (ie current assets)
> and
> *maximise* the amounts owing to creditors and other short term lenders of capital (eg bank overdrafts (ie Current liabilities)

Achieve this aim in the case of:
> Debtors:
> Ascertain financial credibility of customers
>
> Give minimum credit period
>
> Permit minimum credit outstanding beyond credit period
>
> Monitor collection procedure
>
> Stock:
> Decide minimum stock levels
>
> Monitor stock usage and recording procedures
>
> Dispose of obsolescent stock quickly
>
> Creditors:
> Establish rules for opening supplier accounts
>
> Check order procedure
>
> Negotiate maximum credit
>
> Negotiate longest credit period

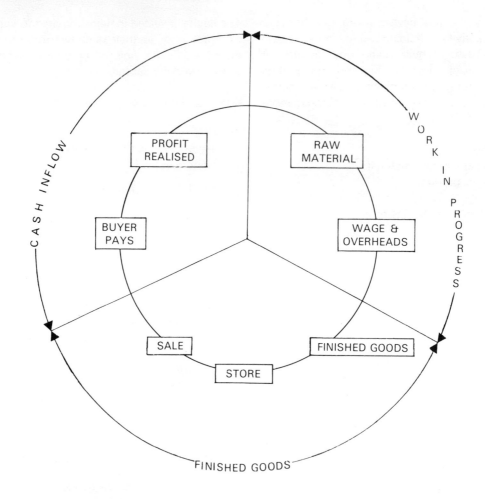

The above illustrates the cycle for manufacture of a single product. In reality the company is engaged in a series of manufacturing processes both of different articles and time spans, for example:

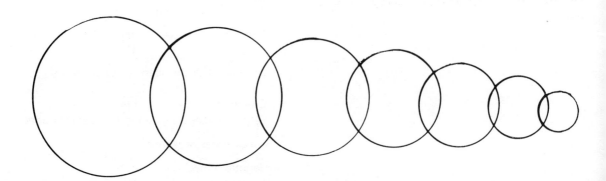

Strategic:
    operate more quickly
    increase individual responsibility
    overhaul the information system
    encourage management participation at all
    levels

Tactical:
    manage business to maximise cash flow in
    short term
    introduce more effective cash control
    systems
    attempt larger and more effective cash fore-
    casting techniques

Immediate Aims:
    speed up cash flows
    delay cash outflows
    minimise delays in clearing funds to central
    bank
    sell to third parties rather than internal cus-
    tomers
    buy from other group companies where
    possible
    establish departmental or company targets
    for cash reduction exercise
    do not recruit staff except for vital tasks
    consider staff utilisation generally
    review minimum stock levels
    determine total stock levels
    analyse slow moving stock
    convert redundant stock into cash
    ensure maximum credit terms obtained from
    suppliers
    curtail unnecessary capital expenditure
    delay unnecessary revenue expenditure
    where no safety or health hazard is involved
    keep debtor investment to minimum
    consider 'cash with order' for new customers
    set off debtor and creditor accounts where
    possible

'Overtrading' is trading in a way which results in proprietors or shareholders' investment no longer carrying all the risks.

If the net cash flow is insufficient to pay creditors, fixed assets might have to be sold to raise the money. This may mean the end of that business as a going concern.

Overtrading through ignorance or incompetence leads to financial resources being over-strained. This may show itself in over-investment in fixed assets, excessive credit being given or taken, the production cycle taking too long, inadequate planning of marketing and selling and an ineffective response to competitors (causing falling sales and lower margins).

Overtrading deliberately is all too often an unavoidable financial tactic (in the early stages) for a company wishing to expand fast and take full advantage of the opportunities open to it. In some cases, though, it comes as a considerable surprise when record profits are accompanied by a cash shortage. This arises through profits being confused with cash. They are, of course, entirely separate. Finance is about cash, and cash is normally required to support growth and higher profits — not vice versa. In rectifying the subsequent illiquidity, there are three points to take into account:

Sufficient time must be allowed to seek out and negotiate the appropriate new capital. This may take up to four months. If insufficient time is allowed, acute financial pressure can put the management in a weak bargaining position. Quite apart from this, financial institutions dislike being rushed and faced with emergencies; such an environment can make them very nervous and disinclined to invest.

The management must be able to demonstrate financial competence.

Running out of money is a sign of bad management and no financial institution called in at this stage will blithely disregard the warnings.

Analysis of the financing potential should disclose the following:

Present financial position — and its financing potential

Net amount of new money required each year

New assets requiring finance and whether or not they are suitable for money-raising

What cushion required — how the inherent fund-raising capacity of various assets can be initially under-utilised to provide for this contingency in the future

Proportion (gearing) of finance to be provided by the shareholders and other lenders (long, medium and short-term)

Cash which will become available to meet loan repayment obligations

Level of net current assets

Terms of credit granted by suppliers

Credit terms with customers and bad debt record

Seven financial situations:

There are seven financial situations worth distinguishing:

Insolvency — Companies with few assets and excessive debts.

Overtrading — Companies with illiquid assets and immediate debts. In order to survive, bills must be paid, other short-term commitments reduced and liquidity improved.

Expanding — Companies with assets and plans requiring funds for growth.

Worker/Shareholders requiring release of capital in a Non-Public Company

Budding entrepreneurs — Individuals with an idea but insufficient capital of their own.

Inflationary — Stable companies requiring finance to keep going

Management buyouts – existing business or trade purchases by its management and supported by venture capital

Once the financial situation can be broadly classified, likely sources of finance can be identified.

A company seeking finance should know the following:

Purpose

Amount required and planned/possible period of repayment

Likely sources

Facts supporting the request

Long-term objectives based on commercially sound judgements

An application for finance should include:

Estimate of the finance required to meet the company's operating plans

Substantiation of the expected profits

Forecast of the funds available internally and the external requirements

Estimated timing for injection and repayment of borrowed funds. These should be separated into long, medium and short-term requirements, and so distinguished in the cash flow forecasts and projected sources and uses of funds statements. In preparing these figures, the business must be thought of in terms of cash not profits

Four financial documents are required in support:

The opening (actual) and projected balance sheets throughout the relevant period

Summarised projected trading accounts for that period

Cash flow forecasts supporting the balance sheets and profit and loss accounts

Previous audited accounts

7.40 BANKERS/LENDERS CRITERIA

Prior to seeking finance, a case containing certain information must be prepared to include:

Description of firm, history of achievements

Description of management structure and senior management

Summary of previous five years financial data (if available)

Copy of most recent audited accounts ideally along with relevant management accounts, control and monitoring procedures

Summary of major influences on the profits and cash flow

Summary of technical ability

Summary by product classifications, order book, market and market share

Detailed projections for period covered by new financial requirements together with basic assumptions on which projections prepared. A note of the downside and upside risks is always helpful together with detailed cashflow projections

Amount of finance required, repayment schedule and security offered (if any)

Borrowers must NOT:

Procrastinate over repayment

Fail to honour credit arrangements

Gamble a way out of trouble

Borrowers must choose bankers who will display a sense of participation in the borrowers business. Personal chemistry, trust and support is essential to ensure an effective banking relationship.

7.41 INSURANCE

Responsibilities of Insurance Manager:

Identification of risks and recommendations

Appropriate cover

Maintaining insurance covers

Making recommendations on risk improvement

Handling claims

Maintaining communications within company and with external insurers and advisers.

Maintaining adequate records

Maintaining constant review of company policy regarding levels and types of cover

Ensuring Insurance Manual is kept up-to-date

Insurance Manual — contents:

Corporate policy on insurance

Responsibility for insurance matters

Brief description of insurance covers

Procedure for communicating catastrophy or other accident

Procedure for claim notification and settlement

Personnel policies affecting employee insurance

Valuation procedures, professional advisers and incorporation of revised valuations.

Maintenance of fire fighting and prevention equipment

Protection of records

Advantages of insurance brokers:

Wide knowledge of insurance market

Specialised knowledge and expertise

Access to all insurance markets

Prestige as intermediaries

Assistance in negotiating premium rates and the settlement of claims

Independent surveying services

Worldwide representation

7.42 COMPANY ACQUISITIONS

How strong is the product range of Company X?

Are competitors likely to become more effective in the near future?

Are the markets for the products of Company X growing or declining? How and why?

Will Company X still be successful for the foreseeable future?

Stages in acquisition:

Exploration   Proposition
Screening   Negotiation
Investigation   Integration

Key pitfalls:

Failing to place responsibility at a sufficiently high level

Failing to establish a real unanimity of opinion as to what the acquisition objectives should be

Setting unrealistic criteria for today's competitive sellers' market

Searching only among companies for sale

Failing to recognise the time required for a successful acquisition programme

Failing to focus the search correctly

Failing to investigate prior to actual negotiations

Failing to assess correctly a seller's motives

Overlooking opportunities by using mechanical screening procedures

Failure to obtain qualified outside assistance when needed

Too much analysis and too little action; or vice versa

For a successful acquisition programme:

Establish clearly defined growth objectives

Establish acquisition criteria

Establish highly creative effort with appropriate supervision

Note: Improved control of early stages of programme will result in significant savings in time and money.

7.43 MERGERS

Special considerations:

The objectives of a merger must be defined in advance before the assessment takes place. A plan in relation to the organisation, management, marketing and manufacturing policies of the merged company must be known or prepared in the course of the appraisal, to avoid misunderstanding about what is intended and how it is to be achieved.

The management style of the two companies must be explored and compared.
Potential leaders of the combined management team must be identified.

Merger checklist:

What is the acquisition strategy of the company initiating the merger?

Does the company being appraised fit the defined specification?

Does it fit the parent?

Does the management style of the two companies fit?

Is there enough management talent?

Is the merger to eliminate product competition or simplify the combined product range?

Is a monopoly situation created and if so what conditions must be satisfied?

To what extent will rationalisation of production facilities be possible?

Can a saving be achieved in administration overheads?

Is the position relating to raw material supplies strengthened?

Does the combined organisation attract greater purchasing power?

What is the effect of the merger on the trading operations situated abroad?

Are there any political conditions to be satisfied in the overseas territories?

What financing arrangements are necessary prior to and subsequent to the merger?

What Stock Exchange requirements must be fulfilled?

Have profit forecasts been made for the combined company?

What is the benefit to the ultimate shareholders in terms of earnings per share?

Franchising is a safer way to establish a business for oneself but not by oneself.

Before agreeing to a franchise, the franchisee (the person who will operate the business) should enquire:

Has the business of the franchisor been proven?

Can examples of business success be visited?

Is discussion with existing franchisees encouraged?

Will the franchisor grant use of an established name, patent or copyright?

Will the franchisee benefit from large scale advertising programmes?

Will a contribution to costs of the advertising programme be agreed in advance and will this contribution be onerous?

What training is offered by the franchisor both for the product and business management generally?

Will assistance be given regarding site selection, supply of equipment and what will be the cost?

Is the basis of remuneration acceptable?

Is it intended that detailed procedure or operating manuals will be made available?

Are boundary limits agreed relating to geographical and product area?

Is there likely to be public demand for the product?

Will there be competition in the immediate area of operation both in quality and price? (source of supply of product or raw material must be considered and is an optional source available?)

Will the rights and obligations be clearly defined in a written contract?

On what basis can the format of the operation be changed?

Will the franchisor have the right of intervention and will the grounds be clearly defined?

What profit expectations can be expected?

What capital requirements are to be anticipated?

Does the intending franchisee have the right personal skills to run a business, the profit of which in the start up years will be paid to someone else?

Examine the credibility of the franchisor:—

Check the length of time the franchisor has been in business

How many franchisee operations does he have?

Check with trade associations eg British Franchise Association

Obtain bank reports and annual accounts

Consider what the consequences are if the franchisor ceased to trade

What arrangements apply if the franchisee wishes to sell the business voluntarily or of necessity?

What is the term of the agreement and provision for renewing?

Does the franchisor welcome the use by the proposed franchisee of independent legal and accounting advice?

8 Data Processing

8.1 CHOOSING AND INSTALLING A COMPUTER SYSTEM

The question — not "should we have a computer" but "how" and "when".

Key factors affecting a computer acquisition:

Is senior company management involved with the project of choosing and installing a computer?

Has a senior executive been given responsibility for success of the project?

Is it necessary to appoint a day to day Computer Manager or Supervisor?

Without senior management commitment it is probable that the computer system will fail

Specify the requirements of the computer system:

Is a computer system feasible?

Can it be cost justified?

Has the relevant system been fully specified?

What are the likely system volumes, average and maximum, in respect of input, output and reference files eg. customer and suppliers records?

What are the time constraints around the key systems?

8.2 EVALUATING THE VENDOR

How long has the vendor been in the computer systems business?

How many computer systems has the vendor installed?

What customer references can be produced?

What kind of experience does the vendor have with computer systems in your type of business?

How many service and support locations does the vendor have?

Is the vendor committed to the computer industry?

What services does the vendor provide?
installation
user training
backup systems
maintenance
documentation
conversion services
program support
others

Does the vendor quote all costs? (Hardware, software, supplies, training, system installation, maintenance, etc.)?

How much responsibility does the vendor assume for the following:
pre-sale systems analysis
post-sale systems analysis
system configuration
system installation
software installation

Is the installation schedule realistic?
hardware delivery and installation
applications software installation and testing
system design and approval
operator training
conversion of existing records

Is a realistic time buffer built in for detecting and correcting errors?

Does the vendor provide a maintenance schedule?

What are the terms of the vendor's warranty?

Will the vendor take responsibility for the entire system it installs?

Can demonstrations be arranged?

Central Processing Unit (CPU):

How much memory does the CPU hold? Is it sufficient to handle the programs you will run?

Can more memory be added after system installation?

Does the CPU use MOS or core memory? (Core memory does not lose data should the system lose power. MOS [semi-conductor] memory, less expensive than core memory, should include a "battery backup" protection feature to prevent data loss.)

Does the CPU include an automatic restart capability in case of power loss?

Can sections of one program be protected from unauthorised access?

Does the CPU require a "clean room" environment or a raised floor for cabling, extra humidity control and air conditioning equipment?

Can the CPU be protected from unauthorised access? (i.e. does it have a lock and key; can a password scheme be easily implemented?)

What type of electrical power does the CPU require? Can it easily be installed in your environment?

Does the system support diskettes, hard discs, or both types of data storage?

How many diskettes can be used at once?

How many million characters (megabytes) do the hard discs hold?

How many hard discs can be used on one system?

Can different sized hard discs be used on the same system?

What is the maximum amount of data storage the system will support?

Are the data storage units available from a single vendor?

Can data storage units be added at any time after system installation? At what price?

Are the hard disc surfaces removable, fixed, or can both types be used?

Does the system support a magnetic tape unit for backup?

Is the magnetic tape unit industry-compatible?

Workstation or Video Display Terminal (VDT):

How many workstations can the system support?

Can workstations be added at any time after system installation?

Can multiple workstations process multiple tasks?

How many characters can be displayed on the screen at one time?

What operator oriented comfort features does the workstation have?

What ease of operation features are included?

Are international character fonts available?

Can the workstation be located far enough from the computer to suit your needs?

Does each workstation require its own specially designed desk or table?

Is a 10-key numeric (adding machine) keypad standard or optional?

Can the system support more than one printer at the same time?

Can different type printers be used concurrently?

How fast do the character printers operate?

Are international character sets available?

What character features are available?

What operator features are available?

Can the printer access stored data like a workstation?

How far from the computer can a printer be located?

Can the printer provide a hardcopy of data displayed on a workstation?

Can the printer operate simultaneously with the workstation?

Can a printer be added at any time after system installation?

Can the printer provide multiple copies? Will it fit your forms?

8.4 POST VENDOR SELECTION

Has responsibility for the computer project been assigned?
How can senior management be kept in touch with the project?
Is there a plan for the whole project?
What is the critical path on such a plan?
Who is masterminding the operation?
How are user departments to liaise with one another and the computer department?
What are the roles to be played by each user requirement?
What supplies are necessary — stationery, storage etc.?
Financing computer equipment:
    immediate purchase
    leasing
    supplier rental
A cashflow analysis:
    equipment costs
    maintenance costs
    software/application costs
    support costs
    space costs (one-time and on-going)
    other onetime costs
    on-going operating costs
Major problems with computer implementation:
    how can the new system be parallel-run against the existing system?
    does the new system fulfil all its requirements?
    do any temporary links need to be made to existing systems?
    do the new systems need phasing in?
    what systems tests can be made prior to parallel-running?
    what training is needed for the users and computer department?
    what space is necessary to house the computer?
    does the computer require special environmental conditions?
    does it require an isolated power supply?

8.5 EVALUATING THE FINANCIAL CONSIDERATIONS

Typically a vendor quotes hardware, software and systems study costs. But don't forget to ask about:
    programming for your business' special requirements
    training costs (including travel, hotel, meals, materials and lost employee time)
    creating new printed forms
    special system start-ups
    installing systems at remote locations
    special leasehold improvements (such as office partitioning, additional space, air conditioning, special flooring, new power lines)
    installation of ancillary services, such as dedicated telephone lines
    consulting fees
    personnel recruiting
    conversion costs (including data preparation, data conversions and parallel operations costs like equipment, supplies and personnel)
    accountant and legal fees
    on-going costs
    hardware maintenance
    finance charges
    additional space rental or construction
    energy consumption
    supplies (including forms, paper, ribbons, mass storage disc packs and magnetic tapes)
    personnel (such as operators, programmers, managers), including salary and fringe benefits
    insurance
    backup and archival data storage media (tapes, discs, diskettes) and storage space
    future hardware and software upgrades

8.6 WHAT FORM OF COMPUTERISATION SHOULD BE USED?

A local bureau
A national bureau incorporating on-line terminals
A time sharing facility
The responsibility given to a computer systems house to develop and/or run your own computer equipment, i.e. Facilities Management
An in-house computer system run by company staff

In-House/Out-House Processing

Do you trust an external facility?
Do they safeguard the confidentiality of your systems?
Do you wish to have the responsibility of developing, running and supporting your own computer facility?
Do you wish your accounting systems to be controlled internally?
Can additional workloads and sudden demands be better handled in-house or externally?
Can the application packages, if initially run on an external bureau, be transferred ultimately to an in-house machine and at what cost?
Is independence the aim?
What is the most cost effective solution?

8.7 THE ULTIMATE TEST

The data processing activity must be run like a business within a business

The activity must be measured in accounting terms — if it cannot be measured it cannot be managed

Data Processing Managers must be held accountable

9 Business Survival Plan

ACTION the following:

General:
  establish a management structure to suit immediate crisis
  define accountability
  keep grouping small
  identify cost centres and budget accordingly — no matter how broad
  bring into the organisation a feeling of identity — link output to cost control

Information:
  establish a broad cash flow budget (or forecast)
  sharpen up production of control information
  monitor control — relate actual performance to budget
  break down information flow to practical smallest parts
  decide critical factors in organisation:
    cash flow
    production
    orders
    cost control
    customer service
    product development
  highlight main issues in information flow

Relations:
  consider staff discussions and announcements (fact is better than rumour)
  hold regular accountability meetings — but not so many as will interfere with technical aspects of business
  consider announcement and contact with important customers
  consider fully with the company's bankers the proposed plans against cash flow and cash needs
  at all costs keep control and avoid panics

Personnel:
  a halt to recruitment
  transfers to other jobs
  short-time working
  redundancies
  a temporary halt to wage and salary increases other than those already negotiated
  re-examination of inessential employee benefit costs

Order Book:
  set targets and type of work required

Sales/Production:
  complete orders with least cash outflow
  set target for production and work done by value
  investigate deviations from plans; identify whether arising from:
    resources or
    technically advanced equipment beyond capability of company's resources
  consider deposits or payments with orders
  consider approach to customers with purpose-built equipment on order — could they pay for work done to date?

Manufacturing Costs:
  decide levels of expenditure, apply control and monitor
  look for bottlenecks in production
  consider payment of damages where lossmaking orders are involved
  don't struggle against the impossible
  cut out own manufacture if equivalent product available externally
  plan to reduce costs by:
    design changes (value analysis)
    use of a different machine combination
    a more rapid production cycle
    better use of capacities
    shift to other production centres or departments
    transport: more suitable containers, shorter routes
    different processes (casting instead of turning)
    less waste, rejections, overtime, waiting times
    less employees, particularly assistants

lower purchasing prices

contracting instead of own production, or vice versa in some cases

lower consumption of energy

standard products instead of specials

reduction in standard, predetermined times

production interlinking or flow –

production instead of batch production

preventive maintenance

utilisation of waste

suitable tooling kept in good working order

reduction of production overhead costs

use of other materials (plastics instead of non-ferrous metal)

Fixed Cost:

list all fixed costs and aim to reduce by an agreed and practical percentage where possible

Variable (Controllable) Cost:

list areas of cost, aim to reduce by 5–10% on a crash economy basis

link all costs to budgets and to individuals

Capital Expenditure

embargo all capital expenditure

where essential — lease equipment

sell surplus assets — every £1 is a contribution towards the cash deficit

Research and Development

mothball all development but against a limited time — say 9 months

scrutinise future product requirement

Stock:

establish effective control and liaison with production function

control ordering and delivery

run down to acceptable levels of part numbers and values

get rid of "surplus to immediate" requirements where practicable

Debtors:

ensure customer invoicing prompt

ensure cash collections prompt

ensure all cash receipts banked promptly

consider factoring good debts for immediate cash release

Creditors:

ensure best terms are obtained and payment dates are kept

no payments to be made in advance of agreed terms

consider discussing with major suppliers a payments moratorium

Essential:

prepare a survival plan and state simply

set out crisis objective — make sure of full commitment from all staff

establish a practical short-term structure

give individuals responsibility

decide on course of action and timetable; ensure no deviations, but plan must be flexible

take bankers into confidence

establish cashflow information

take staff into confidence on plan — show leadership and confidence that problems can be surmounted

monitor all aspects of plan — on-time effective guessing is better than too-late factual data

get outside professional help in areas where required

Index